Septuagint: Solomon

Septuagint, Volume 17

SCRIPTURAL RESEARCH INSTITUTE

Published by Digital Ink Productions, 2024

Copyright

Septuagint: Solomon

Second edition. December 20, 2024

Copyright © 2024 Scriptural Research Institute.

ISBN: 978-1-998636-12-9

The Septuagint was translated into Greek at the Library of Alexandria between 250 and 132 BC.

This English translation was created by the Scriptural Research Institute in 2020 through 2024, primarily from the Codex Vaticanus, although other Septuagint manuscripts were also used. The translation of the Psalms of Solomon was based on Septuagint manuscript 149, and the analyses of earlier translators, including A. Carrière (Latin, 1870), O. von Gebhardt (German, 1895), H. B. Swete (English, 1899), and A. Rahlfs (Latin, 1935). Additionally, the Leningrad Codex, Aleppo Codex, Dead Sea Scrolls, and Aramaic Targums were used for comparative analysis.

The image used for the cover is an artistic reinterpretation of "The Judgment of Solomon" painted between 1605 and 1613 by Antoon Claeissens.

Table of Contents

TABLE OF CONTENTS

TABLE OF CONTENTS

TABLE OF CONTENTS

TABLE OF CONTENTS

Forward

In the mid-3rd century BC, King Ptolemy II Philadelphus of Egypt ordered a translation of the ancient Israelite scriptures for the Library of Alexandria. This translation later became known as the Septuagint, based on the description of the translation by seventy translators in the Letter of Aristeas. The original version, published circa 250 BC, only included the Torah, or in Greek terms, the Pentateuch. The Torah is the five books traditionally credited to Moses, circa 1500 BC: Cosmic Genesis, Exodus, Leviticus, Numbers, and Deuteronomy.

It is generally accepted that there were several versions of the ancient Israelite scriptures before the translation of the Septuagint, and that it was translated from an Aramaic copy, something which the Hasmonean High-Priest/Kings objected to. The final version of the Septuagint was published in 132 BC, and included the books of Proverbs, Ecclesiastes, Song of Songs, and Wisdom of Solomon within the Wisdom Section of the Septuagint, while the Psalms of Solomon were added as an appendix later, sometime in the 1st century BC. It appears to have been translated between 200 and 140 BC from Aramaic translations.

The book of Proverbs is generally attributed to King Solomon, who is explicitly referred to as the author of some of the proverbs. A number of proverbs are known to have been copied from older collections of proverbs, most notably the Wisdom of Amenemope, which was apparently written by Amenemope son of Kanakht sometime before Pharaoh Akhenaten, circa 1350 BC. The Wisdom of Amenemope, also called the Wisdom of Amenemopet, was an Egyptian New Kingdom Era piece of wisdom literature that is generally considered a masterpiece within the genre. The Wisdom of Amen-emope was rediscovered by Egyptologists in 1888, after being lost for around 2400 years. Subsequently, eight partial copies have been found with dates ranging between 1069 and 500 BC.

Several early Egyptologists noted similarities between Proverbs and Wisdom of Amenemope, culminating in Adolf Erman's 1924 paper that compared the two texts, and pointed out that the confusing verse in the Masoretic version of Proverbs 22: halo chatavti lecha [shilshovm] (shalishim) bemov'etzot vada'at (הֲלֹא כָתַבְתִּי לְךָ [שִׁלְשׁוֹם] (שָׁלִישִׁים) בְּמֹועֵצֹת וָדָעַת) is very similar to a verse in chapter 30 of Wisdom of Amenemope, and the Hebrew verse makes more sense if the Hebrew text had a trans-lation error. This error is now accepted by most major Christian denominations and has resulted in Bibles from the late 20th century onward having the verse "Have I not written for you thirty sayings of counsel and knowledge," instead of "Have not I written to thee excellent things in counsel and knowledge," which was found in the King James Version. As the Greek translation has a significantly different verse from the Hebrew, it is clear that the translators at Alexandria did not understand the Hebrew text either, which implies that the error was also present in the Aramaic translation.

Like the Greek translation, the Hebrew translation of Proverbs appears to have been mostly made from an Aramaic text, however, some terms in the Hebrew text are not found in the Greek translation and are not Aramaic, but Canaanite, supporting the idea that the Hebrew version of Proverbs was at least partially translated from an older Judahite copy of Proverbs, which almost certainly predated the Aramaic translation. The classical form of Hebrew was standardized under the Hasmonean Dynasty, between 140 and 37 BC, which ordered all the older Judahite and Aramaic copies of the Israelite scriptures to be translated into Hebrew. Under Babylonian, Persian, and Greek rule of Judea, the Aramaic language and script had slowly supplanted the older Canaanite language and Phoenician script, and therefore, no one understood the new translations of their holy books, resulting in the creation of the Aramaic language Targums, which explained the new Hebrew text to the Aramaic speaking people of Judea.

In many cases the Septuagint is closer to the Targums than to the Hebrew translations, suggesting that the Targums may have largely been based on the same older Aramaic texts that the Septuagint was translated from. In the case of the Masoretic version of Proverbs, there is at least one word that does not appear to have been in the Aramaic text the Greeks translated, as it is not Aramaic. The word is thmŭt (תהמות) in the Aleppo Codex and tehomot (תְּהֹמְוֹת) in the Leningrad Codex. The Greek translation was abyssous (ἀβυσσοσ), meaning abyss or depths, which is a Greek translation of the Aramaic word thŭmå (מְהוֹלְא), however, would translate into Hebrew as tehom (תְּהוֹם). The word found in the Masoretic text is a feminine form of tehom (תְּהוֹם), and the name of the ancient Semitic goddess of the depths, water, and creation, recorded as Tiamat (𒀭𒋾𒀀𒆳) in Akkadian Cuneiform, and Thmt in Ugaritic Canaanite (𐎘𐎎𐎚). She was widely worshiped during the Bronze Age, but disappeared from Canaanite religion in the early Iron Age, indicating this proverb dates to that era.

In Mesopotamia, the goddess became less important in the Iron Age but was still revered as one of the ancient creator deities. When the Greeks ruled Mesopotamia, they translated her name as Thalattê (Θαλάττη), which means the translators at the Library of Alexandria were working from an Aramaic text that did not include her name, and read thŭmå (𐤍‎𐤕𐤄𐤅𐤋𐤀‎ / **אֻרוֹמָה**), meaning depths, instead of thmŭt (**תְּהֹמוֹת**), meaning Tiamat. Her name was probably removed when the Aramaic translation was made in ancient Samaria, and as the Hebrew translators would not have added an ancient goddess to the Aramaic text they translated, it indicates that not all of Proverbs was translated into Hebrew from Aramaic, and some verses might have been retained in the older Phoenician script (Judahite or Samaritan). So far, no Canaanite fragments of Proverbs have been found among the Dead Sea Scrolls, however, only two fragments of Proverbs have been found among the Dead Sea Scrolls, suggesting it was not a popular text.

As archaeologists have yet to find evidence that King Solomon existed, he is generally considered to be a fictional character by most historians, however, the fact that the Book of Proverbs attributed to him includes quotes from an ancient Egyptian source does lend some credibility to his being a historical person. According to the Septuagint's 3rd Kingdoms (Masoretic Kings) and 2nd Paralipomenon (Masoretic Divrei ha-Yamim), Solomon's first wife was the daughter of the Pharaoh, which is generally viewed as a marriage of alliance, as the Canaanite town of Gezer (in modern Israel) was transferred to Israel with her.

Given the traditional dating for Solomon's reign of circa 970 to 931 BC, she could only have been the daughter of Pharaoh Usermaatre Amenemope who reigned between circa 1001 and 992 BC, King Aakheperre Setepenre Osorkon the Elder who reigned between 992 and 986 BC, or King Netjerkheperre-Setepenamun Siamun who reigned between 986 and 967 BC. Pharaoh Amenemope was the last of the native Egyptian Pharaohs, and Osorkon the Elder was the first of the Libyan (Meshwesh) dynasty. The Libyan dynasty appears to have used Egyptian princesses as bargaining chips, also marrying off Karimala to the Nubian king to secure their southern border, however, it is unclear if the princesses were part of the native Egyptian line or Libyans. The marriage described in 3rd Kingdoms and 2nd Paralipomenon appears to be consistent with the Libyan treatment of the Nubians from the archaeological record, supporting the idea that a similar marriage took place in Israel. The author, whoever it was, appears to be very depressed about the state of their life, which does seem likely if she was the last of the former royal family of Egypt, who had been married off to a barbarian king.

As the time period in question falls during the Third Intermediate Period (dark age) in Egyptian history, there is no record of Solomon within the very limited Egyptian records from the time either. Nevertheless, there are few records of anything in any detail from the time period in Egypt or Canaan. Egyptologists believe the Kingdom of Egypt collapsed at the beginning of the time period, and by the time that Solomon would have lived, in the 10th century BC, the king of Egypt only controlled the northern region, while the rest of Egypt was under the rule of the High Priest of Amen (Amun).

As King Osorkon the Elder's reign over Egypt was likely cemented via marriage to a surviving native princess, it seems likely that he and his successor, King Siamun, would have used any other surviving members of the native regime as bargaining chips, as described in both the Hebrew texts and the Nubian relief that mentions Queen Karimala. This indicates that the unnamed wife of Solomon was the daughter of Pharaoh Amenemope, who would have most likely carried a copy of the Wisdom of Amenemope into Israel with her. The name Amenemope seems to have been quite common in ancient Egypt, and it is unlikely that the pharaoh was named after the scribe who wrote the Wisdom of Amenemope, but, no doubt an Egyptian princess would have taken something to give her new barbarian husband, and a book called the Wisdom of Amenemope, with a name identical to her father's would have been a valuable gift. Given that Solomon appears to have quoted part of it, it seems to be where he got the idea to write a book of proverbs, similar to the ancient Egyptian custom, which by his time was disappearing.

The book of Ecclesiastes is generally attributed to King Solomon, however, he is not mentioned anywhere by name. Within the book the author is mentioned as being someone called the Ecclêsiastou (Ἐκκλησιαστοῦ) in Greek, meaning approximately "female cleric," and Kohelet (קֹהֶלֶת) in Hebrew, possibly meaning "female member of the community." The Masoretic term probably originated in the Egyptian term qåỉ ḥnůt (𓂝𓄿𓆑 𓈎𓏏 𓊢), meaning "high queen," suggesting the author was Solomon's first wife. If qåỉ ḥnůt were transliterated directly into Canaanite in the era of Solomon, it would have been qhnt (𐤒𐤄𐤍𐤕), which could have been rendered as qhlt (קהלת) by mistransliterating an N (𐤍) as an L (𐤋).

The current view of the academic community is to regard the book as a Persian or Greek era text, something that dates to long after the time of Solomon. There is no consensus among academics as to whether it is a Persian or Greek era text, and views are largely biased by the researcher's view of the text, and whether it looks like it is more influenced by Plato or Zoroastrianism to that specific researcher. In all fairness, the text's constant references to the dichotomy of light and darkness is similar to some of Plato's work, as well as the central conflict within Zoroastrianism of light versus darkness, however, the constant mentioning of "everything under the Sun" could equally point to an Egyptian influence of Amen-Ra worshipers, Atum devotees, or even Atenists. Moreover, the philosophical view of the texts, in which the toil of this life is seen as insignificant in comparison to the life in heaven, is far more in tune with Egyptian New Kingdom era philosophy than Greek or Persian philosophy, indicating that the text may well date back to the time of Solomon.

As most major Christian denominations now agree that the Proverbs "of Solomon" include proverbs influenced by the ancient Egyptian text called the Wisdom of Amenemope (or Instructions of Amenemope), there is a clear precedent for New Kingdom era Egyptian wisdom literature influencing the works traditionally associated with King Solomon, and therefore, there is no reason to rule out Ecclesiastes as dating back to circa 950 BC. As archaeologists have yet to find evidence that King Solomon existed, he is generally considered to be a fictional character by historians, however, the fact that the Book of Proverbs attributed to him includes quotes from an ancient Egyptian source does lend some credibility to his being a historical person.

The Song of Songs appears to be love poetry, exchanged between Solomon and one of his wives, however, it is not clear who exactly the wife was. The wife describes herself as black, suggesting a Kushite woman. She also refers to herself as a Shulammitess, and makes clear she was not from Jerusalem. The town of Shunaam was located near the Jezreel Valley north of Mount Gilboa, in the tribal lands of Issachar at the time. It was also listed as one of the towns conquered by the Egyptian Pharaoh Thutmose III circa 1450 BC, and then again by Pharaoh Shoshenk I circa 925 BC, meaning there was a significant town was there for over 500 years. It was the hometown of King David's last concubine, the 12-year-old Abishag, who Adonijah attempted to marry after David's death, which suggests the author was Abishag the Shulamite.

If this song was the work of Abishag, it means that it would date to the time of Solomon, and imply she was one of Solomon's wives or concubines. The geography of the Song of Songs is curious, as it seems focused on northern Israel and southern Lebanon, not Judah. Jerusalem is mentioned repeatedly but as part of the phrase "daughters of Jerusalem," which is a group the author clearly does not see herself as being a part of. This suggests that she was living in the north, possibly in the palace Solomon built in the mountains of Lebanon, and saw the daughters of Jerusalem as her rivals for his affection.

The Wisdom of Solomon was added to the Septuagint sometime between 250 and 132 BC, and while it was traditionally attributed to King Solomon, this book was never copied by the Masoretes, and no fragments of it have been found among the Dead Sea Scrolls, indicating it was not used much in Judea, if at all. A Syriac version of it is included in the Peshitta, the Syrian Orthodox Bible, which the Syrian Orthodox Church has always claimed was transcribed from the Aramaic text that the Jews translated into Hebrew, however, most modern scholars believe the Peshitta was a Syriac translation of the Septuagint.

As a result, Wisdom of Solomon is a text that cannot be proven to have existed earlier than 132 BC, when it appeared in the Septuagint, and some scholars have concluded it was written in Greek at the Library of Alexandria. Wherever it was written, it is a very heretical Israelite text, which contradicts, and occasionally even attacks the Torah. These contradictions are often interpreted as indicators that the writer was not particularly knowledgeable regarding the Torah, suggesting a Hellenized Jew, and therefore, it is generally assumed the book was written shortly before its inclusion in the Septuagint. All of these assumptions are, of course, based on the underlying assumption that Judaism was already standardized before the Greek Era. The books of Maccabees tell a very different story.

2nd Maccabees claims to be an abridged version of Jason of Cyrene's now-lost five-volume version of Maccabees written during the Maccabean Revolt of 165 through 140 BC. Jason's work appears to have not been focused on the Maccabean Revolt itself but told the history of Greek Judea up until the time of the Maccabean Revolt, which began in 165 BC. When Judas the Hammer was recognized as the high priest of Jerusalem by King Antiochus in 164 BC, he is recorded in 1st Maccabees as tearing down the altar in the Second Temple, which had been profaned, and building a new one. Clearly, whichever god had been worshiped in the temple in the years immediately before 164 BC was not Judas' god. In 2nd Maccabees, the god's name is translated into Greek as Dionysus (Διονυσίων), which Greek records from the era record as being the Greek name of the Judean god Sabaoth (Σαβαώθ). Sabaoth was also recorded as being the Judean version of the Roman god Bacchus, and the Phrygian god Sabazios (Σαβάζιος), both of which were regarded as the local versions of Dionysus by the Greeks. It is worth noting that while the Greeks considered the Phrygian god Sabazios the local equivalent of Dionysus, the Phrygians considered Sabazios the equivalent of Zeus, the ruler of the Greek pantheon.

The governor of Jerusalem between 168 and 164 BC was recorded as being Philippon the Phrygian in 2nd Maccabees, who considered Sabaoth to be the equivalent of the Phrygian Sabazios and Greek Zeus, meaning that the god that Judas was purging the temple of, was a Sabaoth-Sabazios-Dionysus-Zeus composite god, which no doubt seemed very alien to the Judahites not living in Jerusalem. The Maccabean revolt was not led by urban Judeans, but rural Judeans, as recorded in 1st and 2nd Maccabees, and specifically by the Levite family of Jason, meaning it was a religious revolution, intended to restore the god the rural Judeans of the era were worshiping. This god was recorded as Yhŭ (וחי) in Aramaic, and Yhŭh (𐤉𐤄𐤅𐤄) in Phoenician, the two scripts commonly used in Judea at the time. The Greeks translated the name as Iaô (Ιαω), and the Romans translated it as Iaw, both derived from the more common Aramaic version of the name, which was used from Mesopotamia to Egypt.

The popularity of Yhŭ among the Israelites of the Persian era is well established archaeologically, by his being one of the main Judean gods worshiped at the Israelite temple in Elephantine (modern Aswan). He is mentioned, along with his wife Anat, in the 5th century

BC Elephantine papyri, some of the oldest surviving Israelite texts. The Elephantine papyri date to a span of approximately 100 years, between roughly 520 and 420 BC, and include texts in many languages that were rediscovered in the 1800s and 1900s near Aswan, where an ancient Persian fortress once stood guarding the southern frontier of Egypt against a Kushite invasion. While the Elephantine papyri include many texts in many languages, including hieratic and demotic Egyptian as well as Aramaic and Greek, the Aramaic texts are the most extraordinary, as they reveal a group of Israelites who seemed to have been practicing a form of archaic Judaism and yet knew nothing of the Torah. Arthur Cowley, the Head of the Bodleian Library at the University of Oxford, described what the texts revealed in 1923:

> "So far as we learn from these texts Moses might never have existed, there might have been no bondage in Egypt, no exodus, no monarchy, no prophets. There is no mention of other tribes and no claim to any heritage in the land of Judah. Among the numerous names of colonists, Abraham, Jacob, Joseph, Moses, Samuel, David, so common in later times, never occur (nor in Nehemiah), nor any other name derived from their past history as recorded in the Pentateuch and early literature."

Archaeology has proven the existence of the kingdoms of Judah and Samaria, as both were recorded in the records of Egyptians, Assyrians, and Babylonians, and both left extensive physical evidence of their existence on the landscape of modern Israel and the Palestinian West Bank. Nevertheless, these Israelites in southern Egypt, in the 5th century BC, did not seem to know of Moses or his Torah, meaning that neither could have been viewed as that important to the Israelites at the time. This supports the traditional Jewish belief that Ezra the scribe restored the Torah to its place of importance when he restored Judaism. The dating of Ezra the scribe's life has been debated greatly over the millennia, largely because there were so many Persian kings named Artaxerxes, but also because of the so-called "missing years" of Rabbinical history, in which the Second Temple was built in 352 BC, 70 years after the destruction of King Solomon's Temple in 422 BC. This dating contradicts both the Tanakh (Christian Old Testament) and the Babylonian Chronicles, which both report that King Solomon's Temple was destroyed in 587 or 586 BC.

The Rabbinical timeline is recorded in many early Jewish texts, including the Talmud and Seder Olam Rabbah. Yet, if the Neo-Babylonian king Nebuchad-nezzar II destroyed King Solomon's Temple in 422 BC, instead of 587 BC, and the Babylonian Empire was conquered by King Cyrus 58 years later, that would have been 364 BC. This would then mean the entire span of the Persian Empire was only 34 years long, as Alexander III of Macedon conquered the empire in 330 BC according to Greek records. While Rabbinical sources dispute Alexander's conquest in 330 BC, claiming it was 318 BC, this does not alter the fact that extensive records of the Persian Empire spanning centuries survive in Persian, Greek, Egyptian, and Indian texts.

The establishment of the Second Temple in 352 BC does correlate closely with the records in the books of Ezra, as Ezra the Scribe arrived in Jerusalem in 351 BC, the seventh year of King Artaxerxes III's reign. The question of which King Artaxerxes sent Ezra to Jerusalem has been debated for millennia as well, however, Nehemiah is recorded as being the governor in Jerusalem when Ezra arrived, and Nehemiah reported being sent to Jerusalem in the twentieth year of an Artaxerxes, who recalled him to Persia twelve years later, before he was allowed to return to Jerusalem, meaning that his king had to be Artaxerxes II, the only Artaxerxes to rule for more than 20 years.

Nehemiah had requested to return to Jerusalem to rebuild it after it had recently been attacked, in Artaxerxes II's twentieth year, which was 384 BC. This attack against Jerusalem was likely part of the ongoing war between Persia and Egypt which spanned 404 to 343 BC, as the Egyptians struggled for independence from the Persian Empire. The destruction of Jerusalem in 386 BC, and the destruction of the temple the following year in 385 BC, was predicted by the angel Gabriel in chapter 9 of the Book of Daniel (Theodotion's chapter structure), a chapter which appears to have been added in 385 BC after the temple in Jerusalem had been destroyed.

Nehemiah returned to Jerusalem to rebuild the walls and gates of the city, however, when Ezra arrived decades later, the walls had been torn down again, and the temple was still being rebuilt. As the Second Temple had already been built by Zerubbabel ben Salathiel during the time of Darius II, who ruled between 423 and 404 BC, it is clear there was more than one Second Temple. In 1st Ezra, the Temple was recorded as being completed on the 23rd day of the month of Adar, in the sixth year of King Darius. Zerubbabel's king is often assumed to be King Darius I, also called Darius the Great, who ruled the Persian Empire between 522 and 486 BC. However, as the Artaxerxes is listed as stopping the work on the temple before Darius restarted it, and Artaxerxes I ruled the Persian Empire between 465 and 424 BC, after Darius I, this must be a reference to Darius II restarting the work. Darius III was the last Persian king, who Alexander conquered, and who had already lost control of most of the Empire by 332 BC, the fourth year of his reign, meaning Alexander the Great would have been mentioned instead of Darius if Zerubbabel's temple was completed in 330 BC.

This, therefore, means that there were at least two Second Temples: Zerubbabel's temple completed in 417 BC, and Ezra's Temple, built in 351 BC. While this resolves the issue of why the Rabbis claimed that the Second Temple stood for 420 years, between 352 BC and 68 AD, it does not answer the question of why the Rabbis have ignored the existence of the earlier Second Temple, Zerubbabel's Temple. Both books of Ezra also refer to the captive Judahites being released in the first year of King Cyrus II, presumably 539 BC, and returning to Jerusalem to rebuild the city and its temple under the leadership of Governor Sheshbazzar. Both books, 1st Ezra and 2nd Ezra (Masoretic Ezra-Nehemiah), then skip ahead to "the time of King Artaxerxes," when those living around Jerusalem sent a petition to the king to stop the city and temple from being rebuilt. King Cyrus II died in 530 BC, and Artaxerxes I did not take the throne until 465 BC, meaning that either the temple and city walls were being rebuilt so incredibly slowly that it is a wonder anyone even noticed, or they had been torn down again between the time of Cyrus and Artaxerxes.

In 460 BC, the fifth year of Artaxerxes I, the Egyptians revolted against the rule of the Persians, and the revolt continued for six years until 454 BC. This is most likely when Artaxerxes would have rescinded the earlier orders of Cyrus, to prevent the rebellion from spreading into Judea. The letters found among the Elephantine papyri that had passed between the temples in Elephantine and Jerusalem between 520 and 420 BC, could only have been addressed to a temple that existed before Zerubbabel's Temple was built in 417 BC, and therefore, there must have been an earlier Second Temple, Sheshbazzar's Temple, built after the original Judahites returned from Babylon in 539 BC. This would mean there are two Second Temples that have been ignored by Rabbinical history.

Again, the prophecy of Gabriel in chapter 9 of the Book of Daniel, which appears to have been added in approximately 385 BC, when Jerusalem was destroyed, may shed light on what happened, as it appears to have been a "prophecy" of what had happened during the Persian rule of Judea, ending with the "end of time" in 385 BC. The "prophesies" in chapter 9 begin by stating that Daniel realized that 70 years had passed since the destruction of the Temple of Solomon, meaning it would have been the year 517 or 516 BC. These years are interpreted as weeks for angels, and so Gabriel claims that 70 weeks have passed. He then goes on to make a series of predictions of things that would transpire over the following "weeks," including the arrival of the Savior Abbot (χριστοῦ ἡγουμένου) or Messiah Ruler (מָשִׁיחַ נָגִיד) after 7 weeks, which would have been approximately 510 BC. Apparently, someone in Jerusalem circa 385 BC, considered someone who arrived in Jerusalem in 510 BC to have been the Messiah, or at least to have claimed that title.

The author refers to the year the prophecy was made as the 'first year of Darius the son of Ahasuerus of the descendant of the Medes' in the Codex Vaticanus and Masoretic Text, with Ahasuerus translated as Xerxes in the Codex Chisianus. Therefore, all the codices agree on the names Darius and Xerxes, as Ahasuerus (אחשורוש) was the Hebrew translation of Xerxes. Xerxes (𐎧𐏁𐎹𐎠𐎼𐏁𐎠) is Old Iranian for 'ruling over heroes,' which was translated into Babylonian as Aḫšiyaršu (𒄴𒅆𒅀𒅈𒋗), and then transliterated into Aramaic and ultimately Hebrew as Ahasuerus (אחשורוש). Nevertheless, there was no King Darius who was a son of a Xerxes. Moreover, all the sources also state that this Darius was ruling over the Kingdom of the Chaldeans, which would have been the Babylonian Empire. Seventy years after the destruction of Solomon's Temple was approximately 517 BC, however, Cyrus II had already conquered the Babylonians in 539 BC. Clearly, the author of Gabriel's prophecy was not living at the time it was apparently made, and while he may have understood some of Judea's history under the Persians, he did not understand the early history of the Persian kings.

Gabriel's prophecy continued with a span of 62 weeks, following which the city would be rebuilt, which would have been circa 448 BC. This was year 12 of Artaxerxes I, and six years after he had suppressed the Egyptian rebellion. Gabriel's prophecy continued with another 62 weeks, following which the "anointed one" would be destroyed. This would have been 386 BC and year 18 of King Artaxerxes II. This was the year that King Artaxerxes II betrayed his allies in Greece, and signed a peace treaty with the Spartans, allowing the Spartans to create a hegemony over the Greek mainland. The sudden change of foreign policy was likely because of a shift in loyalties within the Persian court, as he spent the next year suppressing a rebellion among the Cadusians in modern northwest Iran. The following year, year 20 of Artaxerxes II, Nehemiah reports going to Jerusalem to rebuild the walls and gates. This was probably part of Artaxerxes II's new plan to invade Egypt, which he seems to have begun planning as soon as the Cadusians had been defeated in 385 BC.

The Gabriel prophecy implies the Egyptians attacked Jerusalem in 386 BC, as whoever attacked it left the temple standing. There is some circumstantial evidence of an Egyptian invasion in 386 BC, however, thus far archaeologists have not found anything concrete to support the invasion. Nevertheless, the Egyptians were backing the Spartans against the Persians, and so a sudden attack in Judea would have caused Artaxerxes to change plans in Greece. The Gabriel prophecy then predicts the temple being plundered and destroyed the following week, which would have been 385 BC, the year before Nehemiah traveled to Jerusalem to rebuild its defenses. If a temple was destroyed in 385 BC, it would have been Zerubbabel's temple, which had been built in 417 BC.

Nevertheless, 385 BC was not the "end of time," as the Gabriel prophecy predicts, and history continued. Nehemiah traveled to Jerusalem in 384 BC, year 20 of Artaxerxes II, to rebuild the walls of the city, which means that Gabriel's prophecy in chapter 9 of Daniel, had to have been added somewhere in late 385 or early 384 BC. After 12 years in Jerusalem, in year 32 of Artaxerxes II, Nehemiah was recalled to Persia, which was the year 372 BC, after Artaxerxes II's failed invasion of Egypt in 373 BC, and the beginning of the Great Satraps Rebellion, a general rebellion by the governors of the empire which took a decade to resolve.

Both 1ˢᵗ Ezra and Masoretic Ezra refer to Nehemiah by the title of attharias/hattirshata (Ατθαριασ / הַתִּרְשָׁתָא). The word is generally interpreted as meaning something like "governor" in translations of the Masoretic texts, however, it is not the Hebrew, Aramaic, Persian, or Babylonian word for "governor." The Persian word for governor, xšaçapāvan (𐎧𐏁𐏂𐎱𐎠𐎺𐎠) is transliterated in the Hebrew version of Esther as achashdarpan (אֲחַשְׁדַּרְפָּן), which makes hattirshata (הַתִּרְשָׁתָא) an unlikely transliteration. The word that the author was likely trying to transliterate, was the Persian word artshtaran (ارتشتاران) which translates as military "chieftain," or military commander. If Nehemiah was an ethnically Judahite military commander in the Persian army, it would explain why he was sent to build the wall around Jerusalem, and why he left to serve the king during the Great Satraps' Revolt. It also suggests that he returned after the end of the revolt in 362 BC, but before Artaxerxes II died in 358 BC, as Artaxerxes II was the one who appointed him to his position in Jerusalem.

When he returned, his focus had shifted to restoring the faith and unity of the Israelites and removing the unworthy and dishonest from office. This suggests that the region had been somewhat lawless during his absence. Eliashib the priest at the temple, had apparently been stealing the tribute intended for the priests and singers, who had left the temple to work in the fields. Additionally, the Judeans were not observing the Sabbath, but working and trading on that day, which Nehemiah banned in Jerusalem, and then threatened violence against those that conducted business outside the city walls, which confirms that he did have military authority over the city, and the ability to send forces out into the hinterland if necessary. He was also appalled that the Judahites were marrying people from Ashod, Amman, and Moab, and producing half-breed children. He reports that he chased them, cursed them, hit them, and pulled their hair to make them stop, but according to the events that took place during Ezra's time, Nehemiah could not make the Judeans stop marrying strange women.

While the restoration of the Torah is intimately connected with Ezra in 351 BC, from the accounts of Nehemiah, the Judeans were not following it when he returned to Jerusalem, which was likely around 362 BC, although the exact year is not given. Nehemiah may have been sent back to Jerusalem the second time for the same reason as he was previously sent, to rebuild the city's fortifications, as in 351 BC Persia launched another massive invasion of Egypt. This invasion was such a colossal loss that Persia lost control of most of Anatolia, as well as Cyprus, and Phoenicia, but not apparently Judea, where the book of Ezra records he had been promoting xenophobic policies. Ezra's commands, that all the Judean men of Israelite ancestry divorce their non-Israelite wives and abandon their mixed-race children included many ethnic groups, including the Canaanites, Greeks, Perizzites, Jebusites, Moabites, Egyptians, and Edomites, but interestingly, the Persians, Medes, Arameans, Babylonians, and Assyrians, are not mentioned, and none of them were part of the rebellion during Artaxerxes III's reign.

2nd Maccabees, which claimed to be a condensed version of Jason of Cyrene's five-volume history of the Maccabees, stated that Nehemiah had rebuilt the temple, however, as Jason's work was focused on the political history of the Judeans, this was likely the temple built by Ezra in 351 BC when Nehemiah was the governor the second time. 2nd Maccabees includes some strange aspects of the temple that indicate it had been previously used as a Zoroastrian fire temple.

"When our forefathers were led into Persia, the priests that were then devout, took the fire of the altar secretly and hid it in a hollow place of a pit without water, where they kept it safe so that the place was unknown to all men.

Now, after many years, when it pleased God, Nehemiah was sent from the king of Persia, sent from the descendants of those priests that had hidden the fire. However, they told us they found no fire, but instead found thick water. He commanded them to draw it up and to bring it out, and when the sacrifices were prepared, Nehemiah commanded the priests to sprinkle the wood and that which laid on it with the water. When this was done, and the time came the sun rose and lit up the darkness, a great fire was started, so that every man marveled...

...When the sacrifice was consumed, Nehemiah commanded the water that was left should be poured on the great stones. When this was done, a flame was started, but it was consumed by the light that shined from the altar. When this matter was known, it was told to the king of Persia, that in the place, where the priests that were led away had hidden the fire, there appeared water, and that Nehemiah had purified the sacrifices with it. Then the king made the place sacred after he had investigated the matter. The king took many gifts and bestowed on those who he would gratify. Nehemiah called this thing Nephthar, which is as much as to say, purification, but most men call it Naphtha."

Naphtha is a flammable liquid hydrocarbon mixture, produced from natural gas condensates, petroleum distillates, and the distillation of coal tar and peat. In the ancient Persian empire, crude oil was also used as naphtha. Naphtha was used to keep the eternal fires of the Zoroastrian religion burning. The word naphtha, in various forms, had existed in the Middle East for thousands of years by the time this letter was written, and the author appears to be implying the Israelites in Jerusalem had turned it into a sacred term by his time. Petroleum was known to the Akkadians as naptu (𒅖𒈾𒊍), which appears to be the source of the Aramaic neptā (ܢܦܛܐ), Avestan napta (ܢܦܬܐ), Greek naphtha (νάφθα), Hebrew npt (נפט), and Arabic naft (نفط). Naphtha is not mentioned in the books of Ezra, however, an eternal fire is mentioned in relationship with Shesh-bazzar's temple from 539 BC in 1ˢᵗ Ezra, when King Darius had the records search for evidence that the Judahites had permission to rebuild the temple:

> "Then King Darius commanded to search among the records in Babylon, and also in the palace at Ecbatana in the land of Media, where there was found a scroll in which these things were recorded. In the first year of the reign of King Cyrus, Cyrus commanded that the Temple of the Lord at Jerusalem should be rebuilt, where they will sacrifice with eternal fire."

This suggests that Cyrus intended to build a Zoroastrian fire temple in Jerusalem, however, the Elephantine papyri correspondences with that temple do not show any signs of Ahura Mazda being worshiped there, and while several gods were worshiped at the Israelite temple in Elephantine, only Yhŭ is mentioned in the papyri in connection with the temple in Jerusalem.

Therefore, at the time, Yhŭ was interpreted as the Judean version of Ahura Mazda, the Zoroastrian god, which explains why some descriptions of him from the Second Temple Era describe him as being made of fire and brimstone.

This description is nothing like Sabaoth, Dionysus, Bacchus, or Sabazios, all of which had horns, like Yhŭ, but none were made from fire and brimstone. This means that the nice friendly Aramean 'god of desires' Sabaoth, replaced the fire god Yhŭ at some point. The prophecies in Daniel may also shed light on this, as chapter 11 (Theodotion's chapter structure) appears to have been written in Greek, before being translated into Hebrew, and later back into Greek. Daniel chapter 11 contains a prophecy attributed to Daniel which spans the history of the Persian Empire, from Cyrus to Alexander, which most likely originated with High Priest Jaddua's Greek translation of Daniel. The 1st century AD Judean historian Josephus recorded that as the armies of Alexander the Great were advancing on Jerusalem, High Priest Jaddua of the Temple in Jerusalem, took Alexander a copy of the Book of Daniel to show that the Judahites believed Alexander was going to be victorious against the Persians. It is unlikely that they would take him an Aramaic or Hebrew text, or some strange combination of the two languages like the version that survives within the Masoretic Text, and, therefore, it is accepted that Jaddua took Alexander a Greek translation, however, given the number of variants of Daniel it cannot be known for sure what was in that translation.

Chapter 11, which was spliced into the Chapter 10/12 prophecy from the angel Michael, accurately recounts the history of the Persian Empire, ending with Alexander approaching the city and the statement that 'there is none to save him' regarding the Persian king Darius III. Unfortunately, the chapter is written as a prophecy, and so no names are mentioned after the opening lines which state the year the vision was in. The prophecy outlines briefly the rise of the Persian Empire, followed by its break up as the King of the North battled the King of the South, also called the King of Egypt. From the Judean perspective, this was the final century of the Persian Empire, one long war to maintain or regain control over Egypt and Macedonia.

The prophecy accuses both kings of being treacherous and claims the King of the North 'will corrupt the Temple with the god Maozin, whom their forefathers did not know.' Maozin (Μαωζιν) was Theodotion's 2nd century AD Greek translation of the proto-Masoretic word Môzym (מעזים), which is not a Hebrew word, although this chapter of the Masoretic texts is in Hebrew. It is sometimes interpreted as the plural form of "mighty" in Aramaic, however, Theodotion knew Aramaic and did not translate it that way. While Theodotion's translation of this chapter was from Hebrew, the Hebrew name appears to have been transliterated from the Greek word Mazaeon (Μἄζαῖον), the accusative declension of the Greek name Mazaeos (Μαζαῖος). Mazaeos was the Greek form of the Persian and Aramaic name Mazdāya (ך‬ואׂ‬ד‬), which was itself the Aramaic and Persian form of the Avesta name Mazdā (سو٠سۇ6), meaning the god in question was Ahura Mazda, the Zoroastrian god. However, the term surviving in the Masoretic Text does not read Mazdāya (ךדוא / מזדי), the Aramaic and Hebrew version of the name, indicating this chapter was written in Greek and then translated into Hebrew.

As Juddua was the High Priest just 20 years after Ezra had restored the Talmud, it seems unlikely this corruption of the temple with Ahura Mazda was during that brief period, moreover, there are Rabbinical records from that era, meaning it was either the Temple of Sheshbazzar from 539 BC, or the Temple of Zerubbabel from 417 BC.

This also contradicts Rabbinical History, which records that Shaltiel, the father of Zerubbabel, was the first exilarch (ראש הגולה), or "prince in exile," of the Judahites that were taken to Babylonia by King

Nebuchadnezzar in 597 BC. This would make Shaltiel the son of King Jehoiachin of Judah, who was born in approximately 616 BC, yet his son Zerubbabel was alive 200 years later, in 417 BC. While it is clear that a line of succession has been traced back to Shaltiel, he could not have been the grandson of King Jehoiachin, however, based on the Gabriel prophecy in Daniel, may have been the "anointed one" who died at "the end of time" in 385 BC.

Shaltiel is not the only first exilarch of the Judahites recorded. Strange "end of the world" texts also exist from another, supposedly earlier exilarch who lived in Babylonia before the Persians conquered it, an exilarch named Ezra. This was not Ezra the scribe from the late Persian era centuries later, although that Ezra may have been named after this one. This one is called Ezra the Prophet, to distinguish him from Ezra the Scribe, although the two are often confused anyway. Ezra the prophet was associated with a very strange messianic branch of the Israelite religion, and the author of the Judahite Apocalypse of Ezra. In it, he was taken away to a strange place in the sky, quite unlike later early Jewish and Christian ideas of heaven, but somewhat like descriptions of the planet Vaikuntha in the Hindu Bhagavata.

The Judahite Apocalypse of Ezra claims to be one of many books of Ezra the prophet, however, only two others seem to have survived to the present, the Latin Apocalypse of Ezra, and the Syriac Apocalypse of Ezra. Additionally, the Greek Apocalypse of Ezra and Vision of Ezra were associated with Ezra, although they likely descend from a Christianized ancient Egyptian text. The Greek Apocalypse of Ezra is certainly a Christian era work, dated to anywhere from the 2nd to 6th centuries AD, however, the Judahite Apocalypse of Ezra is considered pre-Christian, and of unclear origin. It describes the coming of a Messiah that would unite all of Israel from across the world, build a mountain in Jerusalem, and then stand on top of it and shout fire and lightning at the nations of the world until they all submitted to the rule of Jerusalem. It was incorporated into early Christian Bibles as the 4th Book of Ezra, however, generally dropped long ago as whatever Messiah it was predicting was not Jesus.

While there is no evidence that the author of the Judahite Apocalypse of Ezra was the son of King Jehoiachin, this has been the view of the Ethiopian Orthodox Church, which still includes the book in their Bible. If this is correct, then it may explain why an exilarch was associated with the return to Jerusalem in 539 BC, however, unless he lived for centuries, it could not have been Shaltiel. Nevertheless, Shaltiel's son Zerubbabel was described as attempting to restore the

Judean monarchy in Rabbinical literature, although how he did this while Judea was part of the Persian Empire is not discussed. It seems apparent that he would have needed to revolt against Persian rule to accomplish this, and yet no revolt is recorded unless he was the "anointed one."

The prophet Haggai was alive during Zerubbabel's time and claims to have been the prophet who told Zerubbabel that the Lord Almighty (Κύριοσ παντοκράτωρ) wanted the temple rebuilt. His statements regarding the second year of Darius match the records in the books of Ezra the scribe, and in that year Haggai reported having a series of visions from the Lord Almighty, promoting the rebuilding of the temple, however, his final vision suggests that the Lord Almighty did want Zerubbabel to rebel from Persian rule:

> "The word of the Lord came the second time to Haggai the prophet, on the twenty-fourth day of the month, saying, "Speak to Zerubbabel the son of Shealtiel, of the tribe of Judah, saying, 'I shake the sky, and the earth, and the sea, and the dry land. I will overthrow the thrones of kings, and I will destroy the power of the kings of the nations, and I will overthrow chariots and riders, and the horses and their riders will come down, everyone by the sword striving against his brother. On that day,' says the Lord Almighty, 'I will take you, Zerubbabel, the son of Shealtiel,

my servant,' says the Lord, 'and will make you as a sigil, for I have chosen you,' says the Lord Almighty."

The term "Lord Almighty" is the common translation of the Greek Cyrios pantocratôr (Κύριοσ παντοκράτωρ), which translates as approximately "Lord All-powers." The term was used as a translation of Shaddai (שַׁדַּי) in the Masoretic books of Bereshít (Cosmic Genesis), Names (Exodus), and Job. The book of Bereshít mentions the god Shaddai as the god of Abraham, Isaac, and Jacob. The term Shaddai appears 48 times in the Masoretic text, with 31 occurrences in the book of Job, 6 in Bereshít, and once in Names when Moses' god introduced himself as the god of Jacob and then revealed his name as Ôn (Ων) in the Septuagint's version of the verse. It seems that the references to Shaddai in Cosmic Genesis and the identity of Ôn in Names have been edited, as there is no mention of Shaddai in Cosmic Genesis, and no reference to Ôn in Names.

The name Saddae (Σαδδαι) was also transliterated into Greek once in the Septuagint's book of Ezekiel, indicating that the god Shaddai was still worshipped until around 700 BC. In Aramaic texts that were translated into Greek, the god was called "the god of Abraham, Isaac, and Jacob," suggesting the name was suppressed. The name disappears entirely in the Hebrew texts after Babylon conquered Judah, suggesting the suppression of

Shaddai took place during the reforms of the Judean king Josiah shortly before the Babylonian conquest. The Septuagint's Book of Haggai uses the term Pantocratôr (Παντοκράτωρ) where the Leningrad Codex uses Tzeva'ot (צְבָאֹות). As the Book of Haggai was written circa 520 BC, this indicates the shift in terminology likely took place earlier than 520 BC.

The prophet Zechariah, who prophesied at the same time as Haggai in the second year of Darius, when Zerubbabel was rebuilding the temple, prophesied from Lord of forces (Κυρίου τῶν δυνάμεων) in the Septuagint's translation of Zechariah. However, the Leningrad Codex used the term Yehvah tzeva'o (יְהֹוָה צְבָא) instead of Yehvah tzeva'ot (יְהוָה צְבָאֹות), suggesting it was translit-erated from the Aramaic ådny ṣbå (ܐܝܪܝ ܐܢܕ), meaning "Lord of Desire," instead of the Phoenician ådn ṣbåůt (𐤕𐤅𐤀𐤁𐤑 𐤍𐤃𐤀), meaning "Lord of Forces." As the transla-tors at the Library of Alexandria worked from Aramaic texts, the Aramaic texts probably used the terms ṣbåůt (צאבות) and šdy (ܫܕܝ) interchangeably. Zachariah's work also ends with a prophecy of the end of the world brought on by the Lord of forces:

> "It will happen on that day that there will be no light, and there will be for one day cold and frost, and that day will be known to the Lord, and it will not be day nor night, but towards evening it will be light. On that day living wa-

ter will come forth out of Jerusalem, half of it towards the former sea, and half of it towards the latter sea, and so will it be in summer and spring.

The Lord will be king over all the earth, on that day there will be one Lord, and his name one, compassing all the earth, and the wilderness from Geba to Rimmon south of Jerusalem. Ramah will remain in its place. From the gate of Benjamin to the place of the first gate, to the gate of the corners, and to the tower of Hananel, as far as the king's wine presses, they will live in the city, and there will be no more any curse and Jerusalem will live securely.

This will be the overthrow with which the Lord will strike all the nations, as many as have fought against Jerusalem, their flesh will consume away while they are standing on their feet, and their eyes will melt out of their holes, and their tongue will consume away in their mouth..."

The author of 2nd Maccabees wrote a long preface to his abridged version of Jason's work, which spans the first two chapters. It contains a number of references to Moses, Solomon, Jeremiah, and Nehemiah that are not found in the surviving versions of the various books about them. The author of 2nd Maccabees clearly viewed Nehemiah's religion as being a continuation of the ancient religion of Moses and bridged the two by telling a story about Jeremiah, who found a secret temple of Moses in the caves of Mount Nebo, in modern Jordan.

The tabernacle, box of the covenant, and the altar of incense were hidden there, however, the Greek text does not make it clear if they were hidden there by Jeremiah, or if he found them hidden there. It is generally assumed the story was written as a claim that he hid them there, after saving them, somehow, from the Babylonians who had destroyed King Solomon's Temple, and most of the city of Jerusalem. As Jeremiah was imprisoned in Jerusalem throughout the siege and considered a heretic, it is difficult to imagine how he would have got his hands on the most sacred relics of the temple, and as the story is not found in the other books attributed to Jeremiah, or Baruch, his scribe, it is generally dismissed as a late addition, likely in the era of the Maccabees, with no historical merit.

Nevertheless, the quote in 2ⁿᵈ Maccabees contains a curious term which is neither Greek, nor Aramaic, but Phoenician, suggesting that the text the author was quoting was either something written in the era of Jeremiah when Phoenician was the script of the Kingdom of Judah, or, something written by a Samaritan, as the Samaritans continued using the Phoenician script throughout the Assyrian, Babylonian, and Persian occupations of Samaria. The term in question is in the middle of the phrase 'topos cathagiasthê megalôs' (τόποσ καθαγιασθῆι μεγάλωσ), which in Greek means, 'place cathagiasthe greatness.' The word in the middle of the sentence is not Greek or Aramaic, but a transliteration of the Phoenician term htgyyśty (𐤆𐤕𐤅𐤆𐤆𐤕𐤄), meaning "he chose." This means the sentence originally read "place he chose for greatness," in a Phoenician source text.

The term is in a quote of Jeremiah's meaning the quote was taken from a Phoenician copy of a book or letter attributed to Jeremiah. There were many books attributed to Jeremiah and/or his scribe Baruch in the Second Temple era, including the Septuagint's Book of Jeremiah, Peshitta's Book of Jeremiah, Masoretic Book of Jeremiah, Book of Baruch, Lamentations, Letter of Jeremiah, 2nd Baruch, Syriac Apocalypse of Baruch, Letter of Baruch to the Nine and a Half Tribes, Greek Apocalypse of Baruch (3rd Baruch), Paralipomenon of Jeremiah, and Meneo 4th Baruch. Some of these books are attributed to Jeremiah in one language, and Baruch in another language. Translations of the various books have survived in Armenian, Greek, Hebrew, Syriac, Old Slavonic, Ge'ez, and Romanian, but not in Phoenician. Nevertheless, Jeremiah was in Jerusalem before the Babylonians conquered the Kingdom of Judah, and so would have been writing in the Phoenician script. This story does not appear in any of the surviving books of Jeremiah or Baruch, which means there was at least one other book or letter attributed to Jeremiah in Judea during the Greek Era.

The purpose of the author's retelling of the story of Jeremiah finding Moses' secret temple in the caves of Mount Nebo, was to support the claim that Nehemiah was a great prophet, which, he is generally not interpreted as being by either Jews or Christians. The author of 2nd Maccabees quotes Jeremiah as stating:

> "The place will be unknown until the time when God gathers his people together again and shows them mercy. Then the Lord will reveal these things, and the glory of the Lord will be seen, and the cloud as Moses saw it, and like when Solomon was worthy to see the place he chose for greatness."

The author of 2nd Maccabees is clearly trying to link the temple cave of Moses, to the place where the sacred fire was hidden when the Persians took the Judahites away to Persia. This is itself a contradiction, as the Persians are generally seen as the liberators of the Judahites and Samaritans that had been held in the Babylonian and Median Empires. Nevertheless, many Judahites were reported to have been working for the Persians, which suggests that not all of them were allowed to return in the time of Cyrus II. However, before the Persian era, there was no evidence of an eternal fire being used in Jerusalem. Eternal fires were used in Zoroastrian fire temples, and, like the eternal fire the author describes, used naphtha and asbestos. Nehemiah does appear to have been more of a Zoroastrian than a Judahite and may have tried to re-establish a Zoroastrian fire temple in Jerusalem. If so, he is likely the origin of the story that the author is referring to, in which the sacred fire was hidden when the Judahites were taken to Persia.

The author of 2nd Maccabees appears to be trying to justify Nehemiah, by linking Moses' encounter with the fire god of Mount Horeb in Exodus, Solomon's encounter with the genies from folklore, and Jeremiah's finding of Moses' secret cave temple, where, he implies, the sacred fire had been stored with the rest of the relics from Solomon's Temple, although, what he quotes does not state that the sacred fire was with the rest of the relics. Only the encounter between Moses and the fire god of Horeb is considered canon to Judaism and Christianity, although Solomon's encounters with the genies, a group of fire beings, did end up in the Quran. The Testament of Solomon, likely an early Christian-era work, retold the story from Jewish folklore, however, made the genies into demons. In Jewish folklore, Solomon had commanded genies to build his palace in the Anti-Lebanon mountains, which is similar to, and likely based on, the much older Ba'al Cycle story from the late

Bronze Age, in which "fires" worked for six days to build the Temple of Ba'al on Mount Zephon.

The author of 2nd Maccabees' promotion of Nehemiah as a great prophet, and the sacredness of fire, suggested a surviving Judean sect that was influenced by the Zoroastrian-Yahwist religion of the early Persian Era as late as the 2nd century BC. 2nd Maccabees is also the most avidly anti-Dionysus/Sabaoth text in the Septuagint, indicating that the author did not see Sabaoth as just another name of the true Judean fire god, but a foreign impostor.

Given the complex religious history of the Second Temple Era, and the fact that none of the Israelites in Elephantine appear to have even heard of Moses in the 5th century BC, the Wisdom of Solomon does not seem out of place or anachronistic at all, and dismissing it based on contradictions with the Torah seems completely invalid. The Wisdom of Solomon itself appears to have been redacted before the Greek translation, as the first half is about the spirit of wisdom, Sophia in Greek, who is credited with actually doing most of what God (or Yahweh in the Masoretic texts) was credited with doing in the Torah, however, this changes abruptly to crediting the Lord in chapter 11, and Sophia disappears entirely from the rest of the book. Chapter 11 was also the beginning of what scholars call the 'history' section of the book, which generally retold the history found in the Torah up until the exodus from Egypt, however, with some differences. One significant difference was the identification of the Lord as the Sun in chapter 16:

> That which was not destroyed by the fire, being warmed with a little sunlight, soon melted away, so we might know, that we must give thanks to you, the Sun, and pray to you at dawn.

From the Codex Vaticanus:

> ΟΠⲰⲤ ⲄΝⲰⲤΤΟΝ ΗΙ ΟΤΙ ΔΕΙ ΦΘΑΝΕΙΝ ΤΟΝ
> ΗΛΙΟΝ ΕΠ ΕΥΧΑΡΙⲤΤΙΑΝ ⲤΟΥ ΚΑΙ ΠΡΟⲤ
> ΑΝΑΤΟΛΗΝΦⲰΤΟⲤΕΝΤΥΓΧΑΝΕΙΝⲤΟΙ·

The verse is either evidence of an older book than generally assumed, or, a mistranslation by the translators in Alexandria. If it is evidence of an older version of the book, it would support the idea that it originated with Solomon, or someone from the era before King Josiah's reforms banned the worship of the sun-god Shemesh, as well as the Lord (Ba'al), and Asherah, and the army of the sky. This is described in detail in the Septuagint's 4th Kingdoms (Masoretic Kings) chapter 23:

> The king commanded Hilkiah the high priest, and the priests of the second order, and those who kept the door, to bring out of the temple of the Lord all the vessels that were made for Ba'al, and for Asherah, and all the army of Shamayim, and he burnt them outside of Jerusalem in the fields of Kidron, and took the ashes of them to the Temple of El. He burnt the sacred male prostitutes, who the kings

of Judah had appointed, and those who burnt incense in the Bamahs and in the cities of Judah, and the places around Jerusalem, and those that burnt incense to Ba'al, Shemesh, Yarikh, the Zodiac, and the power of the armies of Shamayim.

He carried out the Asherah from the Temple of the Lord to the brook Kidron, burnt it at the brook Kidron, ground it to powder, and threw its powder on the sepulchers of the sons of the people. He pulled down the Palace of Qetesh that was by the Temple of the Lord, where the women wove tents for the Asherah. He brought up all the priests from the cities of Judah and defiled the Bamahs where the priests burnt incense, from Geba even to Beersheba.

He pulled down the house of the gates that were by the door of the gate of Joshua the ruler of the city, on a man's left hand at the gate of the city. The priests of the Bamahs did not go up to the altar of the Lord in Jerusalem, and they only ate leavened bread among their brothers. He defiled Tafeth which is in the valley of the son of Hinns, constructed for a man to cause his son or his daughter to pass through the fire to Moloch. He burnt the horses which the king of Judah had given to Shemesh in the entrance of the Temple of the Lord, by the treasury of Nathan the king's eunuch, in the suburbs, and he burnt the Chariot of Shemesh with fire.

The altars that were on the roof of the upper room of Ahaz, which the kings of Judah had made, and the altars that Manasseh had made in the two courts of the Temple of the Lord, the king pulled down and forcibly removed from there and threw their dust into the Brook of Kidron. The king defiled the temple that was near Jerusalem, on the right hand of the mountain of rubbish, which Solomon king of Israel built to Astarte the abomination of the Sidonians, and to Chemosh the abomination of Moab, and to Moloch the abomination of the Ammonites. He broke in pieces the steles, completely destroyed Asherah, and filled their places with the bones of men. Also, the high altar in the Temple of El, which had been built by Jeroboam the son of Nebat, who made Israel sin, even that high altar he tore down, and broke in pieces the stones of it, and reduced it to powder, and burnt Asherah.

Josiah turned aside, and saw the tombs that were there in the city, and sent, and took the bones out of the tombs, and burnt them on the altar, and defiled it, following the word of the Lord which the prophet spoke...

There is some evidence in the Secrets of Enoch and the other books of Enoch for the continuation of the early Israelite star-worship cults in early Persian-era Judea, which could point to a later origin for the second half of the Wisdom of Solomon, between 587 and 422 BC, during the so-called missing years of Rabbinical history. There is also some evidence in the Revelation of Metatron, Ascension of Moses, and Talmud, that the Jews reverted to worshiping the 70 or 72 Elohim of the ancient Canaanites, which could be why more than a century and a half of Jewish history appears to have been expunged from Rabbinical history. The 72 Elohim were interpreted as small star constellations at one point, however, it is equally possible that the revival of the star cults had taken place under Babylonian rule, and were still fading away in the early Persian Era.

In the Ascension of Moses (chapter 17) the 72 "princes of the sky" are introduced, "Over them are 72 princes of kingdoms in the heights, corresponding to the 72 languages of the world." In chapter 26 of the Revelation of Metatron, Samael was listed as the Prince of Rome, and Dobiel was listed as the Prince of Persia. For some reason, the Israelites and Judahites had different Princes, as Michael was the Prince of the Israelites, while Gabriel was the Prince of the Judahites. While the Princes were occasionally mentioned until the medieval era, most references to them, date to the Persian era. These 70 or 72 Princes, depending on the source, are a direct descen-dant of the 70 or 72 Elohim of the ancient Canaanite reli-gion, which appear to have been 72 god-stars, used like the 36-star groups of the Egyptian's decan system of astronomy.

The idea that the Princes were each over one language group of humanity, is a Persian Era interpreta-tion, used to explain why the Medo-Persians had become the dominant language group instead of the Aramaic-

Canaanite peoples. In the Talmud (Yoma 77a) the ascension of the Persians under Cyrus II was caused by the fact that Dobiel had become the dominant angel in heaven because the Master of the Universe had been angry with Gabriel for allowing the Judahites to escape the destruction of Babylon when the Persians conquered it. Dobiel translates as "bear god" and was a reference to the constellation Ursa Major, the northern constellation, as the Persians had come from the north. These star-god angels of the Persian era certainly border on polytheism, or at least hedonism, which may be why so much Israelite history from the era seems to have been removed from Rabbinical history.

In any event, the description of Sophia, the spirit of wisdom in the first half of the Wisdom of Solomon, also borders closely on polytheism and is certainly hedonistic. She is given most of the powers generally associated with God, whether he is the Sun or not, and is described in terms usually restricted to him, such as all-powerful and all-knowing. She is identified as being the Holy Spirit in Orthodox Christianity, which makes her part of the Trinity. This to some extent supports the view of the early Gnostics who viewed Sophia as the twin of Jesus, and the third member of the Trinity. Undoubtedly, they drew at least some of their theology from the Wisdom of Solomon, which appears to have been the only book of the Israelite scriptures to have been circulated separately from the Septuagint and included with the New Testament in the early Gnostic-Christian communities, as demonstrated by the Muratorian fragment, which is a list of Christian books generally dated to between 160 and 170 AD. The Wisdom of Solomon is the only Old Testament book mentioned in the list, and as it is listed, it is clear that these books were not circulating along with the Septuagint, or there would have been no reason to list the Wisdom of Solomon, which was in the Septuagint.

The first half of the Wisdom of Solomon is written like a love poem about the spirit Sophia, which can be read as either a metaphor or a hedonistic declaration. The author is never specifically named as King Solomon, although he is strongly implied. If the first half of the book was Solomon's writing, the hedonistic perspective would have been consistent with his beliefs as recorded in other Israelite texts. The first half of the book does have a lot in common with the Wisdom of Amenemope, which was quoted in the Proverbs of Solomon. If one accepts that Solomon was a real person, this does support the idea that he composed the beginning of the Wisdom of Solomon. The Wisdom of Amenemope was an Egyptian wisdom text that was written by the scribe Amenemope pen Kanakht sometime between 1550 and 1350

BC. It was lost from around 500 BC until it was rediscov-ered by Egyptologists in the late 1800s. It appears to have served as the inspiration for the Book of Proverbs, a fact so well established that some Bible translations are using it to correct some of the garbled text in the Hebrew translation of Proverbs.

The influence of the Wisdom of Amenemope on the Wisdom of Solomon is less obvious, as there are no direct quotes to indicate the author had read Amenemope, however, it does appear to be attempting to copy the ancient Egyptian wisdom literature concept, which even in the time of Solomon, circa 950 BC, was an older form of literature no longer being emulated within Egypt. By 500 BC, the form seems to have generally disappeared within Egypt, and older Egyptian Wisdom literature was no longer being copied. The most recent copies and fragments of the Wisdom of Amenemope date to this era, and are considered poor imitations of the much earlier versions from the New Kingdom Era.

Nevertheless, the influence of Amenemope is only seen in the opening half of the Wisdom of Solomon, which supports the idea that the book was majorly redacted at some point. This redaction would have to be dated to the early-Persian era at the latest, based on the reference to praying to the sun god found in the second half of the book. In the first half, the author states he is going to explain the mysteries of the spirit Sophia (Wisdom), however, this is followed by a general retelling of the history of the Torah, along with a large number of deviations from the Torah, such as the "plague of darkness" and the "death of the firstborn" happening at the same time. During this dark-death plague, the Israelites left Egypt obscured by a cloud, which is also not mentioned in the Torah but were then attacked by their God, for some reason, until the 'blameless man,' who one would assume to be Moses or Aaron, stood among the heaps of dead bodies and calmed 'god' down. These and other deviations from the various surviving Torahs (Masoretic, Septuagint, and Samaritan) indicate that the author may have been using another version of the Torah, and if so, it would date the Wisdom of Solomon to the Persian era at the latest, as the division between the Jews and Samaritans took place during the Persian rule of Judea.

Undoubtedly, the single largest deviation from the Torah is the fact that the author of this book claims the Israelites made up the Torah themselves, which is essentially the opposite of the Torah's claim that either the Lord or Yahweh gave it to Moses. Another significant deviation is the reference to the Israelites worshiping serpents and other beasts, found in chapter 11. According to the Torah, while the Israelites were in the wilderness, they were attacked by serpents, and Moses fashioned a bronze serpent statue that had the power to save those who turned to it. The books of the Kingdoms (Masoretic: Kings) and Paralipomena (Masoretic Diḇrê Hayyāmîm) record that the statue was erected in King Solomon's Temple, where it was worshiped until King Hezekiah had it destroyed around 700 BC.

Chapter 14 includes a long tirade against idolatry, which is difficult to place in the era of Solomon but does fit into the last century of the Kingdom of Judah when both King Hezekiah and Josiah launched iconoclastic campaigns to rid the land of idolatry. The chapter also contains a reference to child sacrifice, which was not banned until the reforms of King Josiah circa 625 BC. Nevertheless, the identification of the lord as the sun, indicates that the second half of the book was not written during the reign of King Josiah, as Josiah had banned sun-worship along with moon-worship. As King Josiah's prophet was his father-in-law Jeremiah, who was from the Levites of Libnah who were Yahwists, it means that King Josiah's god was Yahweh, however, this Yahweh was not the sun god Yhů of the Persian era Temple of Sheshbazzar, nor the moon god Yhů of the Kingdom of Samaria from circa 800 BC. This Yahweh was Moses' god, renamed Yahweh.

In the Torah's book of Genesis, the Israelites settled in northern Egypt during a great famine, after one of the patriarchs, Joseph, had become an official in northern Egypt. He was previously sold to the Egyptians as a slave and ended up married to the daughter of a high priest in the city of On after interpreting the king's dreams. It isn't clear when exactly this would have been, as the Septuagint and Masoretic texts both record that the Israelites had been in Egypt for 400 years when they left with Moses, however, the Samaritan Torah records that they were in both Canaan and Egypt for 400 years before Moses led them from Egypt. Based on the dating in the Septuagint, the exodus happened in approximately 1550 BC, meaning the Israelites had arrived in Egypt around 1950 BC, during the reign of Senusret I the second king of the Middle Kingdom era. In year 25 of his reign, circa 1946 BC, Egypt was devastated by a famine caused by a low Nile flood, which mirrors the famine in Egypt that Joseph prophesied in Cosmic Genesis (Masoretic Bereshít).

Senusret I oversaw many construction projects, as reported in Cosmic Genesis, and confirmed by archeology. He oversaw the rebuilding of the temples of the sun gods in Ỉủnủ (𓉺𓏤𓊖), later known as Åủn (אוֹן) in Hebrew and Heliopolis (Ἡλίου πόλις) in Greek. According to Cosmic Genesis, Joseph married the daughter of a high priest in Iͦůnů, meaning he would have become a high priest following his step-father. This high priest was supposed to interpret dreams, indicating he was the high priest of the lunar god Iͦôhů, explaining why the name Yhůh gained an extra sound in southern Canaan. Senusret I also oversaw the building of the White Chapel in Karnak, which served as the capital building of Egypt during the Middle Kingdom. The name White Chapel is unusual for Egypt, however, is the translation of the name É-Babbara (𒌷𒌋𒌋𒁀), suggesting there were also members of the cult of Sippar influencing the court of Senusret I, which is likely who had the Hieratic translation of the Book of Job at the time.

The city of Iͦůnů was again mentioned in the Septuagint's book of Exodus when the Israelites were leaving Egypt, along with Pithom and Ramesses. The Book of Names only listed Pithom and Ramesses in Names, however, did mention Joseph's father-in-law being Potipherah the priest of On (אֹן) in Bereshít. As the Greek translation of Exodus used a transliteration of the Aramaic Ån (אֹן), instead of the Greek translation of Heliopolis (Ἡλίου πόλις), the name must have been in the Aramaic source text they used. Moreover, the Hebrew translation of Genesis also uses the Aramaic spelling, transliterated into the Hebrew script as Ån / On

(אֵן / אָן) in the Masoretic texts, instead of the Hebrew spelling of Åůn / Aven (אָוֶן / אֹון), proving that the Hebrew text was made from an Aramaic source instead of a Canaanite (Judahite or Samaritan) source.

The cities of Iůnů, Pithom, and Ramesses were the most important cities of the Hyksos Dynasty. The city of Iůnů was the ancient holy city of northern Egypt, where the sun gods Khepri (𓆣𓏤𓊹), Ra (𓇳𓏤𓊹), and Atum (𓏏𓐠) were worshiped, along with Atum's wife Iusaaset (𓄿𓊨𓏏𓆇), and the lunar god Iåhů (𓇋𓂝𓎛𓇳𓏤). The Late Period's city of Ramesses was the site of the Hyksos capital of Avaris (𓉗𓂝𓏏𓊖) at the time, and the city of Pithom (𓉐 𓏏𓐠), identified as the ruins of Tel El Maskhuta, was a major Hyksos Era settlement west of the Nile, along the old Middle Kingdom Era canal, which linked the Nile river to Lake Kem Wer in the Bitter Lakes. The city of Avaris was destroyed when the Hyksos Dynasty was defeated at the beginning of the New Kingdom Era, however, the location was optimum for trade with Canaan, and so the city was rebuilt as Pi-Ramesses (𓉐 𓂋𓏠𓇓𓋴𓋴) in the 1200s BC. By 1060 BC, the branch of the river that Pi-Ramesses was built along had silted up and the city was abandoned. It was later rebuilt a second time as Ramesses (𓂋𓏠𓇓𓋴) in the era of Pharaoh Shoshenq I (943 to 922 BC), and was still a major city when the Torah was most likely compiled into a book including Cosmic Genesis, Exodus, Leviticus, and Numbers, under King Josiah (640 to 609 BC).

The fact that the major Hyksos settlements are all listed when the Israelites left Egypt, supports the Septuagint's dating of circa 1550 BC for the exodus, as that was approximately when the Hyksos Dynasty was defeated by Ahmose I (⚊𓏤𓏤), founder of the 18th Dynasty. During the era, the major gods of Northern Egypt were Iåḥů, who the Ahmose was named after, and Atum, the sun god, also called Amen (𓇋𓏇𓈖𓏏𓏤) in Southern Egypt. During the New Kingdom Era, Amen, as part of the Theban Triad, eclipsed all other gods in Egypt, almost to the point of becoming quasi-monotheistic religion, with a trinity instead of a single god. This religion was focused on the sun god Amen, his wife Mut, and their son the moon god Khonsu. They were mirrored by their North Egyptian counterparts, Atum, his wife Iusaaset, and the moon god Iåḥů, although in Northern Egypt, the moon was not seen as the son of the sun. As Canaan was part of the New Kingdom, there were also Canaanite equivalents. In Baalbek, the Heliopolitan Triad, as the Greeks later named it, was originally composed of the sun god Ba'al, his wife Astarte, and their son Adon.

The Greeks renamed both Baalbek in Lebanon and On in Egypt Heliopolis, meaning 'Sun City' as both were ancient holy cities of the sun god, which the Greeks called Helios. The version of Astarte worshiped at Baalbek does not seem to be the same sea goddess of the Sidonians, and she is generally equated with the Israelite Asherah and Aramean Ataratheh before the Greeks conquered the region, both of which were associated with fertility, but not the sea. As the Sidonian Astarte was viewed as being the Canaanite version of Aphrodite by the Greeks, she was interpreted that way under the Greek rule of Phoenicia, and later as Venus by the Romans. Their son Adon, was considered the Greek version of Dionysus by the Greeks, although there was a shift away from Dionysus to Mercury, the messenger of the gods by the Roman Era, which seems to have happened at the same time as the Maccabean Revolt to the south. The fact that the Greeks viewed both Adon of Baalbek and Adoni Sabaoth of Jerusalem as being local equivalents of Dionysus, suggests they were very similar.

This triad of gods, the Sun Ba'al, his wife Asherah, and their son Adon, appears to have been the same gods worshiped in King Solomon's Temple, based on the records of the reforms by King Hezekiah and King Josiah in the 8th century BC. The records of the reforms report destroying the statue of Ba'al and cutting down the Asherah, as well as burning the chariot of the sun, and killing its horses. Nevertheless, when King Josiah was killed in battle against the Egyptians, and King Necho II of Egypt made Jehoiakim the new king of the puppet state of Judah, 1st Ezra reports that he did it to restore the worship of the Lord. Clearly, this was not Josiah's god Yahweh, and therefore must have been Necho's god Amen. Necho is well documented as a sun-worshiper, as he built many monuments honoring the Southern Egyptian sun god Amen, and Northern Egyptian sun god Atum. Jeremiah, the Yahwist prophet who inspired King Josiah's reforms spent most of the next decade in prison as a heretic before finally being released by the Babylonians when they destroyed the city, as he was too old to be useful as a slave. A few years later, he traveled with a large number of refugees to southern Egypt when the Judahites attempted to revolt from Babylonian control.

The trinity of gods, modeled on the New Kingdom's Theban Triad, but using Canaanite and North Egyptian names and iconography is described in the Torah, however, generally obscured by later dogma. Moses' god, described as being the creator of the world, appears to be the sun god of On named Atum, who was also depicted as being a serpent, like Moses' bronze serpent. Solar serpent iconography is commonly found in the archaeological records of ancient Judah up until the reign of Hezekiah, indicating that Moses' bronze serpent was the statue of Ba'al which Hezekiah destroyed. Likewise, Aaron's golden calf was a statue of the moon god of On, Iåḥu, who was later in the early Iron Age, still viewed as being the calf of Asherah, as the pottery shards found at Kuntillet Ajrud, dating to circa 800 BC prove. Atum's wife was Iusaaset, a fertility goddess, worshiped by planting acacia trees, which were seen as sacred to her. In the city of Iunu, she was also viewed as being a form of Hathor, and the two were both given the title of Lady Hetepet (𓏏𓊵𓏙), meaning Lady of Sacrifices. Hathor was viewed as the cow of the sky, the goddess that nourished the land with rain, and as such was equated with Asherah, the Canaanite ow of the sky, for whom sacred trees were also planted in Judea and Samaria.

Iusaaset, under her title Lady Hetepet, was often described as being the "Hand of Atum," and therefore, the claims that Sophia did what Moses claimed God did, would not have seemed contradictory to someone who viewed Sophia as being the "hand of god." Exodus even claims that God led the Israelites out of Egypt with his "mighty hand," which would seem to be confirmation from Moses that it was Iusaaset who led the Israelites out of Egypt, at least from the perspective of an Israelite in the New Kingdom Era, who viewed Moses' god as Atum, the creator god of Egypt, which Canaan was then ruled by. This would suggest that the early chapters of the Wisdom of Solomon were written very early, shortly after the collapse of the New Kingdom, but when Egypt still had influence in southern Canaan. This would match the era of Solomon's supposed rule over Judea, Samaria, Edom, and Aram, of circa 950 BC, and he was certainly recorded as being influenced by Egypt, as the correlations between Proverbs and the Wisdom of Amenemope seem to prove.

However, it would also mean that the Asherah was the original name used in the Wisdom of Solomon, and was replaced with Sophia at some point. The Greek name Sophia (Σοφία) is, of course, a Greek translation, and the Masoretic texts use the name Chachamot (חָכְמוֹת), a feminine plural indefinite form of chacham (חָכָם), meaning "wise" or "smart." The Aramaic word ḥkm (חכל) likewise meant 'to be wise,' however, the plural infinite implies the meaning 'wisdom,' and the feminine form implies a goddess of wisdom. If the orig-inal text was written by Solomon, the name of the text was probably Wisdom of Solomon, an attempt by Solomon to replicate the wisdom literature of ancient Egypt, and therefore, the name Chachamot, which also shows up in other texts associated with Solomon, as prob-ably taken from the name of the book itself.

The author describes Sophia leading the Israelites out of Egypt and seems to be at odds with the Torah regarding the Israelites worshiping serpents, a clear reference to Moses' bronze serpent statue. It suggests that Sophia / Chachamot was originally the goddess that Miriam was the prophetess of, as she was clearly not the prophetess of Moses' god, which he himself clarified in the Torah when he inflicted Miriam with leprosy for speaking out against Moses.

This story that discredits Miriam appears in Numbers, and while the language of Numbers suggests it is quite old, possibly dating to the late Bronze Age, it does not appear to have been compiled into a book and added to the Torah until King Josiah's reforms of circa 625 BC. Several books, including Exodus, Joshua, and Job show signs of being translated from Cuneiform, however, all the words in the Masoretic version of Numbers can be traced to Canaanite or Aramaic. The story itself seems unrelated to the surrounding text as if it was inserted later, and it may have been added as late as Josiah's reforms, assuming that Miriam was considered a prophetess of Asherah, the Canaanite equivalent of Lady Hetepet Iusaaset. If the early chapters of Wisdom of Solomon were about Asherah, it would have almost certainly been redacted during the 7th century BC, when Asherah worship was twice banned in Judah, meaning that it was already about Chachamot / Sophia by the time the later sections were added in the Persian era.

The early chapters also include the strange statement:

"God created man to be immortal and made him an image of his own immortality. Jealously the slander Mot came into the cosmos."

The name translated as Mot was Thanatos (Θάνατοσ) in the Septuagint, the Greek god of death. The name Thanatos was used throughout the Septuagint when referring to Mot, the Canaanite god of death, a name preserved in the Masoretic texts as Mavet / Mût (מות / מָוֶת). The name was recorded as Mt (𐤌𐤕) in Ugaritic during the Bronze Age, and later during the Iron Age as Mt (𐤕𐤌) in Phoenician, and Mûtå (ܡܘܬܐ) in Aramaic. The variants of the name are generally normalized into English as Mot. Mot appeared many times in the Israelite texts, where he was interpreted as the messenger of death. This led to his Greek translation Thanatos being seen as the early Christian angel of death. The word translated as "slander" is diabolô (διαβόλω), which later came to mean "devil," however, when the text was translated into Greek meant "slanderer."

In the Greek translation of Job, the term diabolô (διαβόλω) was used in places where the Masoretic texts use the term satan (שָׂטָן), meaning "adversary." This suggests that the original text may have referred to Mot as the "contender," a title applied to him in the Bronze Age Ugaritic texts, when he contended with the Lord

(Ba'al) for the rule of Earth. In that battle, Mot was described as a plague ravaging the world, which even killed Ba'al, although the other gods restored him to life, and he went on to defeat Mot. The verse appears to be referencing the Ba'al Cycle, which again would point to an early composition, certainly before Josiah's reforms, and most likely in the early Iron Age.

Like the Wisdom of Solomon, the Psalms of Solomon were not copied by the Masoretes, and no fragments of it have been found among the Dead Sea Scrolls, indicating it was not used much in Judea, if at all. There is also a Syriac version of it in the Peshitta, which the Syrian Orthodox Church has always claimed was transcribed from an Aramaic copy, however, most modern scholars believe the Peshitta was a Syriac translation of the Septuagint.

The origin of the book is unclear and widely debated. The name Solomon is used in this translation, as it is the name used in the Codex Alexandrinus, however, it should be noted that about half the manuscripts use the name Salomôn (Σαλομών) or Salômôn (Σαλωμών) instead of Solomôn (Σολομῶν) or Solômôn (Σολωμών). This could be a transliteration error, however, the name Solomon must have been well known by the time these Psalms were translated into Greek, so the consistent use of the alternate spelling appears to be intentional. It is possible that the translators and scribes who used the alternate spelling did so in the belief that the author of these Psalms was named Salomon, as he certainly could not have been King Solomon.

Psalms of Solomon does not identify someone called Solomon or Salomon within them, other than in the titles of the psalms, which were added later. The identification of Solomon is based on the reference to the son of David in chapter 17, however, in Aramaic and Hebrew, the term "son of David" would identify any male descendant of David. The one thing that all scholars agree on, is that whoever this son of David was, he was not King Solomon. The events in the Psalms of Solomon describe Jerusalem's walls as having been pulled down, and its temple sacked, which is not something that happened during Solomon's reign, however, is something that happened multiple times later in history.

The first recorded sack of the temple was during Solomon's son Rehoboam's reign when King Shoshenq I of Egypt sacked Jerusalem. Psalms of Solomon does refer to a dispute between brothers preceding the sack of Jerusalem, which did metaphorically happen at the time, as another Israelite, Jeroboam, led a secessionist move-ment in Samaria, which broke away from Judah in the fifth year of Rehoboam's reign. According to the books of the Kingdoms (Masoretic Kings), Jeroboam had taken refuge in Egypt during King Solomon's reign and was married to the Egyptian woman Ano. So the attack of King Shoshenq I on Jerusalem was probably a coordinated effort to break Rehoboam's kingdom, which it effectively did with the help of Jeroboam's rebellion.

The reasons for Jeroboam's rebellion are described as being religious in the books of the Kingdoms, as he built temples to a calf god in Bethel and Dan after achieving independence, something abhorrent to the scribes in Jerusalem, who had recorded the event as heretical. Nevertheless, the calf god of Samaria was depicted on the pottery shards found at Kuntillet Ajrud dating to circa 800 BC, and was named Yhŭh (𐤉𐤄𐤅𐤄), the same name as the later Jewish god, meaning that it was the priests of Jerusalem who were worshiping a different god. In the following decades, both the Edomites and the Levite city of Libnah in the borderlands of Judah, Edom, and Egypt, broke away from Judah over religious differences. As the pottery shards found at Kuntillet Ajrud also refer to the "Yhŭh of Teman," which was the capital of Edom at the time, and the later Yahwist Levites that led the reformation of Judah under King Josiah were based in Libnah, it is clear that Solomon's Temple could not have been used to worship Yhŭh at the time.

All of the references to the gods worshiped in the Temple of Solomon before King Hezekiah's reforms circa

700 BC agree that Ba'al and Asherah were worshiped in the temple, along with occasional references to the sun god Shemesh, the moon god Yarikh, the army of the sky, Tamuz, Adonai and Moses' bronze serpent statue Nehushtan. The wisdom literature associated with Solomon, including the Psalms of Solomon, is consistent with this earlier Jerusalem-based religion, and in chapter four the following line is found:

"Let the bones of the lawless lie dishonored in the sight of Shemesh."

The word the Greeks used to translate Shemesh is Hêliou (Ἡλίου), which is both the Greek word for 'sun' and the name of the Ancient Greek god of the sun, Helios. Among the Israelite texts that were translated into Hebrew, the term shamesh (שֶׁמֶשׁ) was used, the Hebrew word for the sun, and a direct transliteration of the name of the Canaanite sun god Šmš (𐤔𐤌𐤔). Shemesh was one of the gods whose worship was banned by King Josiah of Judah circa 625 BC.

A few years later, King Josiah was killed in battle after attacking the Kushite army, and King Necho II of Kush, who at the time ruled Egypt, appointed his son Jehoiakim as the new King of Judah. Jehoiakim was not the only claimant to the throne when Josiah died, his younger brother Jehoahaz had also claimed the throne and held it for three months before King Necho arrested him and restored the rule of law, placing the eldest surviving son of Josiah on the throne. The author of 1st Ezra claimed that after killing King Josiah, King Necho II of Kush restored the worship of the Lord in Jerusalem, and as Necho was a sun-worshiper, recorded in the Egyptian records as worshiping the southern Egyptian sun god Amen, and the northern Egyptian sun-god Atum, the lord whose worship he restored in Jerusalem had to have been Shemesh.

According to the Talmud, King Jehoiakim claimed the only thing that God provided the world with was light, proving that he too was a sun-worshiper. During Jehoiakim's reign, Jeremiah, a Yahwist prophet from the Levites of Libnah, and the architect of King Josiah's reforms was imprisoned in the royal prison as a heretic until the Babylonians destroyed Jerusalem in 587 BC. Five years later, while a captive in Babylon, Jeremiah's scribe Baruch also described his god as being the sun and claimed that his sacred name was Amen, proving that the Judahites taken captive to Babylon were also worshiping the sun, as the Babylonians, Medes, Kushites, and Egyptians were at the time.

Some scholars believe the events described in the Psalms of Solomon date to the time of Necho and Jehoiakim, as Necho also occupied Jerusalem during a dispute between two brothers, and is reported to have pillaged the temple. If the Psalms of Solomon do date to the time of Necho and Jehoiakim, then they may have been composed by the short-lived King Jehoahaz, whose birth name was Šlŭm (שלום), generally transliterated as Shallum, and possibly the source of the alternate spelling of Salomôn (Σαλομών). According to the very limited records of what happened to Shallum, he was taken prisoner to Kush, where he later died, however, it is not clear how long he lived in Kush, or if he was treated as a dignitary or sold as a slave. Nevertheless, if the origin of Psalms of Solomon was among the Israelite community in Egypt or Kush, it would explain why it does not appear to have ever been important in Judea.

The king who had attacked Jerusalem is not identified in the Psalms of Solomon, other than being called a word the Greeks translated as "dragon" (δράκοντοσ). This term was used to translate two terms retained in the Masoretic texts: tannin (תַּנִּין), and livyatan (לִוְיָתָן). Both terms are derived from Canaanite and are found in the Ugaritic texts as tnn (━➤➤➤➤), the word meaning crocodile, and Ltn (|||━➤➤➤), the name of the asterism now known as Cetus. Both the prophets Isaiah and Ezekiel referred to Egypt as "tannin," and as it was to the south of Judah, it was viewed as being governed by Leviathan (Cetus) by followers of the Neo-Babylonian and Persian Era followers of the Judahite star cults, who also viewed

Dobiel (Ursa Major) as the constellation governing the Persians, who were from the north.

Neither King Shoshenq I nor Necho II was associated with dragons or crocodiles in the view of the ancient Egyptians, and so the term was likely based on the idea that Egypt was itself the crocodile. However, while both of these kings did sack the temple during a dispute between Israelites over who should rule, neither is recorded as tearing down the walls of Jerusalem, which had led to some debate as to whether this event was related to one of them, or later. The Babylonian king Nebuchadnezzar II tore down the walls of the city in 587 BC, when he conquered Judah into the Neo-Babylonian Empire, however, it is entirely possible that the former king Jehoahaz (Shallum), was still alive in 587 BC, as he was a young man in 609 BC, and so he may have visited Jerusalem after the Babylonians had destroyed it.

The city was also reported to have been recently destroyed by Nehemiah in 384 BC, following which he traveled to Jerusalem to rebuild the city's walls and gates. It is unclear what had happened in Jerusalem, however, at the time Egypt and Persia were at war, and Egypt, which had declared independence from Persia twenty years earlier, was financing revolutionary movements in Cyprus and Phoenicia. In 388 BC, the Athenians and Egyptians formed an anti-Persian alliance in support of the rebellion of Evagoras I of Cyprus, however, the following year the Persians and Greeks signed a peace treaty, leaving Cyprus and Greek lands in Anatolia as part of the Persian Empire. King Hakor of Egypt continued to support the anti-Persian rebels in Cyprus, Phoenicia, and Anatolia, and in 385 BC, the Persians invaded Egypt, an invasion which ultimately failed, but managed to occupy parts of northern Egypt for 3 years. It is not recorded who destroyed Jerusalem shortly before Nehemiah traveled there in 384 BC, whether it was the Egyptians before the invasion of 385 BC, or the Persians themselves, however, as King Artaxerxes II sent Nehemiah to rebuild the city, it probably wasn't the Persians.

The temple in Jerusalem that had been destroyed was the temple that Zerubbabel had built between 421 and 417 BC, during the reign of Darius II, however, this temple appears to have been monotheistic, and quite different than the temple that the author of the Psalms of Solomon would have been at. The correspondences between Zerubbabel's Temple and the Israelite Temple in Elephantine, Egypt, which were found among the Elephantine papyri, and date to the time of Zerubbabel, only refer to one god in relation to Zerubbabel's Temple: Yhů (𐤉𐤄𐤅). The Israelite Temple in Elephantine was polytheist at the time, and Yhů was worshiped along with his wife Ônt (𝑃𝑌𝑈), generally transliterated as Anat, as well as the sky god Bytålh (𝑇𝐿𝑁𝑃^𝑌), often transliterated as Bethel. As Yhů was the only god mentioned in the letters in relation to the temple in Jerusalem, it is accepted that Yhů was the only god worshiped in Zerubbabel's Temple.

If there was an attempt to restore sun worship in Jerusalem between the time of Zerubbabel and Nehemiah, it is not recorded, nevertheless, someone destroyed the temple by 384 BC, less than 33 years after it was built. There is some evidence that Zerubbabel revolted against the rule of the Persians shortly after opening the temple, claiming to be a son of David, and the rightful king of Judea, however, most of the references to the era are unclear on what happened. Zerubbabel did have two recorded sons, Hananiah, who became high priest after him, and Meshullam, of whom very little is known. Based on his correspondence in the Elephantine Papyri, Hananiah appears to have been a Yahwist, meaning that if the dispute was between these two brothers, Meshullam would have been the author of the Psalms of Solomon.

After Zerubbabel's temple was destroyed, the next temple built in Jerusalem was recorded as the temple of Ezra, which opened in either 352 or 351 BC, depending on the source. Ezra's temple was plundered by the

Roman general Pompey in 65 BC, after besieging Jerusalem for eight months. Many scholars have suggested that this was the event described in the Psalms of Solomon, however, neither Pompey nor the Roman Empire were ever described as being a "dragon" or "crocodile" in any other Israelite texts making this association unlikely. Additionally, the star "prince" of Rome was listed in the Talmud as being Samael, who was also not associated with either dragons or crocodiles.

Pompey's sack of Jerusalem did take place during the dynastic struggle between two brothers, Aristobulus II and Hyrcanus II, over the succession to the Hasmonean throne, which does support the idea that Pompey was the dragon, however, the Hasmonean dynasty also appears to have promoted monotheism, and there is no evidence of sun-worship during their reign. For those that accept the identification of Pompey as the dragon, the Psalms of Solomon are accepted as an anti-Hasmonean or anti-Roman text, however, there is no evidence the Psalms of Solomon have ever been used by Jews, and no fragments of it have ever been discovered among the Dead Sea Scrolls.

Additionally, the Psalms of Solomon contain references to dietary laws that are not consistent with the laws of Moses and suggest the text was used by the Nazarenes. The Nazarenes were an Israelite sect in Judea during the Second Temple era, who ultimately gave rise to Christianity as well as Mandaeism. The exact beliefs of the ancient Nazarenes are not well documented, as the term has been fought over for 1800 years, however, they were mentioned in 1st Maccabees from circa 167 BC, where they were called the Nazarites. Early Christian scholars like Tertullian, circa 200 AD, recorded that the idea that Jesus was from a town called Nazareth as being a Jewish lie, and his title of Nazarene referred to his being a Nazarite. Whatever the truth, at the time there was no town known as Nazareth in Roman Palestine, as Christians had searched for it for over a century. Eventually, they renamed another town, and the story that Jesus was from Nazareth, instead of a Nazarite became the dominant interpretation. Meanwhile, the term Nazarite is still used by Jews for anyone who vows to follow strict adherence to the Torah for some time.

The Psalms of Solomon repeatedly refers to a group of good people called the "lawful," and seems to use the terms interchangeably. Christian translators have often used the term "righteous" instead of "lawful" for religious reasons, however, the Greek term dicaeôn (δικαίων) is properly translated as "lawful." Christian translators generally avoid using the term "lawful" as Christians are not obliged to follow the Torah, and are, therefore "unlawful," and so substitute the vaguer term "righteous." Nevertheless, these Psalms were not written by a Christian, and deserve to be understood in their original context. The usage of the term "lawful" appears to mirror the usage of the term Nazarene (Nazarite) found in historical texts from the Classical period, implying these Psalms were likely Nazarene in origin.

Like the first Christians, the Nazarenes rejected Moses and his Torah, or Aaron and his god Yahweh, making them "Jews by birth" as Josephus described the Essenes in The Judean War, published around 70 AD:

> "For there are three philosophical sects among the Jews. The followers of the first of which are the Pharisees; of the second, the Sadducees; and the third sect, which pretends to a severer discipline, are called Essenes. These last are Jews by birth, and seem to have a greater affection for each other than other sects have." (from Whiston and Maier's 1999 translation of The Jewish War, page 736)

The Roman writer Pliny the Elder mentioned them in his Natural History, published in 77 AD, and stated that they rejected money, and had existed in Judea for thousands of generations. This means they considered themselves descendants of the Canaanites, not the Israelites, and therefore would not have used Moses' Torah, the holy book of the invaders. This, combined with the reference to the rejection of money, has led to the scholarly opinion that Jesus, the Nazarene was an

Essene and that the "poor" who were going to "inherit the Earth" in his prophecy were the Essenes. This correlates well with the Psalms of Solomon, which also reject material wealth. Additionally, the diet of the Essenes and Nazarenes is documented to have been limited to the consumption of plants, fish, and birds, which are described as the food "for every living thing," in chapter 5, implying the author was an Essene/Nazarene.

Psalms of Solomon does not survive in the oldest manuscripts of the Septuagint, however, was once in the Codex Alexandrinus' appendix, from the 5th century BC. The book was ripped out at some point, and only the title survives. So far, only eleven copies of the Psalms of Solomon have been found in ancient Septuagint manuscripts, all dating to between the 11th and 15th centuries, however, scholars generally assume the translation found in the Peshitta was made from a copy of the Septuagint sometime between the 3rd and 5th centuries AD, and that it was in early-Christian era copies of the Septuagint, as there are several references to it found in early Christian writing.

In order to translate this book, Septuagint manuscript 149 from the 11th century has been used as a source, along with various scholarly translations that have been made of the book since it was rediscovered in the 1600s. Unfortunately, there are still damaged portions of text that have not survived in any of the known manuscripts. Most of these gaps are believed to only be a few words. This translation is heavily influenced and indebted to the translations and research of A. Carrière (*De Psalterio Salomonis disquistionem historico-criticam scripsit*), Oscar von Gebhardt (*Die Psalmen Salomo's zum ersten Male mit Benutzung der Athoshandschriften und des Codex Casanatensis*), Henry B. Swete (*The Psalms of Solomon with the Greek Fragments of the Book of Enoch*), and Alfred Rahlfs (*Septuaginta. Id est Vetus Testamentum graece iuxta LXX interpretes, 2 vols*). Additionally, Robert Hann's *The Manuscript History of the Psalms of Solomon* from 1984 was consulted and is recommended as a source for an in-depth comparison of the 11 known ancient Greek manuscripts of the *Psalms of Solomon*. All of these translations, other than Hann's, long preceded the discovery of the Dead Sea Scrolls, and therefore some of the opinions and assumptions are now seen as dated, however, their research did shape the view of these texts until the 1980s when some of the early assumptions began to be overturned due to expanded knowledge of the complexities of Israelite sects of the Second Temple era, as demonstrated within the Dead Sea Scrolls.

This version is not intended as a critical edition, comparing the different surviving versions, but rather an easy-to-read version that restores the *Septuagint's*

Psalms of Solomon as much as possible to the earliest version. When possible, corrections to the Greek translation are also made, as the Greek used in the translation of this book was inferior to the Greek used in the rest of the Septuagint.

The earliest Christians used the Septuagint exclusively, as far as the Israelite scriptures were concerned, and as a result, it is impossible to even understand the chronology of the world they described unless using the Septuagint. It is unclear why the Septuagint, Masoretic Texts, and Samaritan Asatir each contain a different chronology of the world. Adding the Book of Jubilees, and various variations of the Torah found within the Dead Sea Scrolls, there are at least six ancient Judeo-Samaritan chronologies. The Septuagint's Cosmic Genesis includes an additional millennium of human history that was dropped from the proto-Masoretic texts in order to align the creation of the world with the beginning of the age of El, when the constellation Taurus became the marker of the northern vernal equinox, in 3760 BC. The Bull El was the dominant God of the Canaanite pantheon until circa 1700 BC, when Attar the Goat (Aries) and Yam the Sea-Monster (Cetus) fought for domination of the world beneath the sky, ultimately both being replaced by the god of thunder Ba'al Hadad, in the Canaanite Ba'al Cycle.

FORWARD

Traditional Western Christian and Jewish interpretations of the timeline within the Masoretic texts are further hampered by the so-called "missing years" of Rabbinical Time, in which hundreds of years of the Persian Empire are skipped over in order to make the timeline fit into the era since 3760 BC, a problem Christian chronologists have never had as Christianity developed after the astrology of Babylonian-era Judaism had been forgotten.

The earliest Christian Bibles all used the Septuagint, however, by the 4th century some Christian scholars were asked whether they should retranslate the Old Testament from the version the Jews were using, and some even suggested using the Samaritan version. Both suggestions were generally dismissed as heretical, as Jesus and the Apostles had quoted from the Septuagint, even though they had access to the Hebrew version then in use. This argument held in the West until the Middle Ages when Catholic Bibles switched to the Masoretic texts. In the east, Orthodox Bibles continued to use the Septuagint, as they do today. To the south, the Ethiopian Tewahedo Church continued to use the Septuagint, and across Asia, the Thomas Christians and Nestorians continued to use the Septuagint. Only in Western Europe were the later Masoretic texts adopted, abandoning the more ancient Septuagint, on the assumption that the Jews had copied their texts more faithfully than the Greeks had translated them. This assumption was carried forward into the Protestant Churches that broke off from the Catholic Church, and therefore almost all Protestant Bibles use the Masoretic texts for the basis of the Old Testament.

Unfortunately, this means that the earliest Christian writings are generally confusing and ignored by Protestants and Catholics. The earliest Christians of the first and second centuries quoted books that are no longer in the Bible, and as such, their writings are not always understood. *Septuagint: Solomon* is part of a series of 21st century translations aimed at correcting this problem.

One of the problems with academic translations of the Septuagint is the use of unfamiliar names or terms, as the Septuagint was written in Greek, and therefore many names are unrecognizable to modern readers who are used to Hebrew-derived names. This project uses the more commonly understood Hebrew-derived names instead of their Greek translations, such as Canaan instead of Chanaan, and Melchizedek instead of Melchisedec. Common modern names are also used instead of either Greek or Hebrew terms when geographical locations are known, such as the archaeological name Uruk instead of the Greek Orech, or the Hebrew Erech, and the archaeological term Sumer instead of Shinar or Senar. While this

could be argued as not being a correct academic proce-
dure, it does fulfill the goal of making the translation
easy to read and understand.

Proverbs: Chapter 1

The Proverbs of Solomon son of David, who ruled in Israel, to know wisdom and instruction and to perceive words of understanding and also to receive difficult saying and understand true justice, and how to direct judgment, so that he might give subtlety to the simple, and to the young man discretion in understanding. By hearing this a wise man will become wiser, and a man of understanding will gain direction and will understand parables, dark speech, the saying of the wise, and also riddles.

Fear of God[1] is the supreme wisdom, and there is a good understanding of all that practice it. Piety towards God[2] is the beginning of discernment, but the ungodly will set at nothing wisdom and instruction.

Listen, my son, to the instructions of your father, and don't reject the teachings of your mother. For you will receive for your head a crown of graces and a chain of gold around your neck. Son, don't let ungodly men lead you astray, and don't consent to them.

If they should call you saying, "Come with us. Partake in blood, and let us unjustly attack the just men on the earth. Let us eat him alive like Sheol,[3] and remove the memory of him from the earth. Let us seize his valuable property, and let us fill our houses with spoils. Throw your lot in with us, and let us provide a common purse, and let us share one wallet." Do not go with them, but turn away from their paths. Nets are not spread without reason for birds, and they who partake in murder store up evils for themselves, and the overthrow of transgressors is evil. These are the ways of all that perform lawless deeds, for by ungodliness they destroy their own life.

Sophia[4] sings loud in passageways, and in the wide places speaks boldly. She makes a proclamation on the top of the walls and sits by the gates of princes, and at the gates of the city, and boldly says, "So long as the simple cling to justice, they will not be ashamed, but the foolish being lovers of haughtiness, having become ungodly have hated knowledge, and those responsible increase control. Here I will speak to you with my breath, and I will instruct you in my speech. Since I called, and you did not listen, and I spoke at length, and you paid no attention, and you ignored my counsel and disregarded my disapproval, therefore I also will laugh at your destruction, and I will rejoice when ruin comes on you.

Yes, when sadness suddenly comes over you, and your downfall arrives like a tempest, and when tribulation and distress come on you, and when ruin comes on you! When you call on me, I will not listen to you, wicked men will seek me, but will not find me. For they hated knowledge and did not choose to fear the

Lord,[5] nor would they listen to my counsel, but ignored my disapproval. Therefore they will eat the fruits of their own way, and will be filled with their own ungodliness. For because they wronged the simple, they will be slain, and an inquisition will ruin the ungodly. He who listens to me will live in hope, and will rest securely from all evil."

Proverbs: Chapter 1 Notes

1 Codex Vaticanus: theou (ΘΕΟΥ). Translation: god
- Aleppo Codex: Yhůh (יהוה)
- Leningrad Codex: Yehvah (יְהָוֹה)
- Targum to Proverbs: (דַיְ). Translation: the Yhů

2 Codex Vaticanus: theon (ΘΕΟΝ). Translation: god
This section of text is missing from the Masoretic version and Targum.

3 Codex Vaticanus: Aedês (ᴧɪᴅнᴄ). Translation: Sheol
- Aleppo Codex: šåůl (שׁאוּל). Translation: Sheol (or borrowed, Saul)
- Leningrad Codex: šeôl (שְׁאֹור). Translation: Sheol (or borrowed, Saul)
- Targum to Proverbs: šeyôl (שְׁיוֹל). Translation: Sheol (or borrowed, Saul)

Sheol was the ancient Canaanite underworld, which, like the Greek Hades, was sometimes personified.

4 Codex Vaticanus: Sophia (ϲοφιⲁ) Translation: wisdom (or Sophia (the Gnostic angel or aeon)

- Aleppo Codex: ḥkmût (חכמות). Translation: wisdom
- Leningrad Codex: chachemot (חָכְמוֹת). Translation: wisdom
- Targum to Proverbs: ḥokmetā (חָכְמְתָא). Translation: wisdom (or counsel)

The spirit Sophia / Chachemot is mentioned extensively in the books related to Solomon, and normally translated into English as the "spirit of Wisdom." The equivalent term used in the Aleppo Codes in ḥkmût (חכמות), which was rendered as either chachamot (חֲכָמוֹת) or chachemot (חָכְמוֹת) in the Leningrad Codex. The Hebrew term is a feminine plural indefinite form of chacham (חָכָם), meaning "wise" or "smart."

The Aramaic word ḥkm (חכל) likewise meant "to be wise," however, the plural infinite implies the concept of wisdom, and the feminine form implies a goddess of wisdom. The Septuagint's Sophia appears to have been the basis of the Gnostic aeon (or angel) Sophia, as this "Wisdom" is described being sentient. Based on the Wisdom of Solomon, the goddess in question was likely Asherah before a redaction in the 800s BC replaced Asherah with Ḥkmût.

As the term used here denotes a sentient spirit, the Greek Sophia is used in the translation, as there are no records of a Canaanite or Aramean goddess named Ḥkmût. There was a goddess of wisdom during the Persian era named Ônt (ꟼⲩⱴ) who was married to Yhû (ꟼⲛꞀ), the Persian era version of Yhûh. Ônt (ꟼⲩⱴ) was the Aramaic version of Athena (Ἀθηνᾶ), the Greek goddess of wisdom, and likely imported to Phoenician and Aramaic languages as a replacement for Asherah during the Persian era, as she is documented in the late Bronze Age as Atana (𐀀𐀲𐀙) in Linear-B Greek.

5 Codex Vaticanus: phobon tou cyriou (ΦΟΒΟΝΤΟΥ ΚΥΡΙΟΥ). Translation: fear the lord

• Dead Sea Scroll 4QProvᵃ: ûyråt yhůh (וייראת יהוה). Translation: and awe Yhůh

• Aleppo Codex: ûyråt yhůh (ויראת יהוה). Translation: and awe Yhůh

• Leningrad Codex: veyir'at yehovah (וְיִרְאַת יְהֹוָה). Translation: and awe Yehovah

Proverbs: Chapter 2

"Son, if you will listen to my commandment, and hide it with you, your ear will listen to wisdom. You will also apply your heart to understanding and will apply it to the instruction of your son. For you will call it wisdom, and speak your voice in understanding, and if you will seek it like silver, and search diligently for it like treasure, then you will understand the fear of the Lord, and find the knowledge of God.[1] The Lord gives wisdom, and from his presence come knowledge and understanding, and he treasures up salvation for those who walk uprightly. He will protect their way, so he may guard the righteous ways, and he will preserve the path of those that fear him. Then will you understand righteousness and judgment, and will direct all your course correctly.

If wisdom will come into your understanding, and discernment will seem pleasing to your mind, good counsel will guard you, and holy understanding will keep you, to deliver you from the evil way, and from the man that speaks nothing faithfully. Alas for those who forsake right paths, to walk in ways of darkness, who rejoice in evils, and delight in wicked perverseness, and whose paths are crooked, and their courses winding, to bend you far from the straight way, and to have you follow foreign law. Son, don't follow bad counsel from she who has forgotten the teaching of her youth and forgotten the sacred covenant. She has (the god) Mot[2] and his temple, near Sheol with the Earth's axis itself.[3]

None that follow her will return, nor will they find the right paths, for they do not understand the years of life. Had they followed good paths, they would have found the paths of righteousness smooth, for the upright will live on the Earth, and the holy will be left behind in it. The paths of the ungodly will die out from the Earth, and transgressors will be driven away from it."

Proverbs: Chapter 2 Notes

1 Codex Vaticanus: theou (ΘΕΟΥ). Translation: god

• Aleppo Codex: ålhym (אלהים)

• Leningrad Codex: elohim (אֱלֹהִים)

• Targum to Proverbs: ĕlāhā (אֱלָהָא). Translation: god

The terms ålhym (𐤀𐤋𐤄𐤉𐤌) and ålhym (𐡀𐡋𐡄𐡉𐡌) are direct transcriptions of the Neo-Assyrian word elium (𒀭𒈨𒌋𒌝), which by the Iron Age meant "god," indicating that text had previously been written in cuneiform, and was translated into Aramaic or Phoenician during the iron age. During the bronze age, the Old Babylonian word was Alium (𒀭𒈨𒌋𒌝) and referred to a specific god, [deity]An (✶✶) the highest god, and father of the other gods. His Old Akkadian name was derived from the word elûm (𒀭𒈨𒌋), meaning "higher," as the term was intended to convey the meaning of "highest." He was believed to live in the polar region of the sky, where the modern constellation of Draco is located, making him the highest in the sky, around which all the gods (stars) circled.

The term el elyovn (אֵל עֶלְיוֹן), meaning "highest god," was translated into Hebrew in Bereshít Chapter 14, where the Greeks translated it as theô tô ypsistô (Θεω τω υψιστω) in Cosmic Genesis, also meaning "highest god." El Elyon is known to have been a major god of the Canaanites, called ål ůålyn (𐤀𐤋𐤏𐤋𐤉𐤍 𐤀𐤋), meaning "God and Highest" in an Aramaic language Sefire Treaty from circa 750 BC. The Greek translations of Sanchuniathon's Bronze Age writing that has survived to the present, referred to the primordial creator god of the Canaanites as Elioun (Ελιουν), which appears to be the same god. According to Sanchuniathon, Elioun was the highest (υψιστος) god, who made the sky and the land, and the sky and land made the rest of the gods.

During the Old Babylonian and Old Assyrian eras, the gods Marduk and Ashur, the national gods of Babylon and Assyria, replaced the Akkadian Ān as the primary god of the Mesopotamian pantheons, and by the Iron Age, the word elium had come to mean "god," explaining why the Aramaic term ålhym (𐤀𐤋𐤄𐤉𐤌) would have been interpreted as "god," by the Greeks.

2 Codex Vaticanus: thanatô (ΘΑΝΑΤΩ) Translation: death (or Thanatos)

• Aleppo Codex: ål-můt (אל-מות). Translation: god Mot (or death)

• Leningrad Codex: el-mavet (אֶל־מָוֶת). Translation: god Mot (or death)

PROVERBS: CHAPTER 2

• Targum to Proverbs: demota (דְמוֹתָא). Translation: the death

The Hebrew word mût (מות) is generally assumed to be a spelling error of mûût (מוות), meaning "death," however, as the Hebrew script (Assyrian Block Letter form of Aramaic) script did not exist in the time of Solomon, it must be assumed that the earlier Phoenician or Aramaic script was originally used to compose the proverbs. In Aramaic the word was spelled mût (ﬡﬥﬖ), an exact transliteration of the word found in the Aleppo Codex, indicating that the Book of Proverbs was translated into Hebrew from an Aramaic source. Mot spelled variously as Mūtu (◄) in Akkadian cuneiform, Met (𓄿𓅱) in Egyptian, Mata (𓈖𓅱) in Kushite, Mt (𐎎𐎚) in Ugaritic, Mt (𐤌𐤕) in Phoenician, Mût (ﬡﬥﬖ) in Aramaic, Central Atlas Tamazight Mmt (ⵎⵎⵜ), Mûta (ܡܘܬܐ) in Syriac, Mout (ⲙⲟⲩⲧ) in Coptic, Mata (𐦠𐦩) in Meroitic, Maût (موت) in Arabic, and Mot (ሞት) in Ge'ez, was the word for death, as well as the god of death in Canaan. In the Israelite texts, Mot was treated like the angel of death, instead of the god of death. Mot is well documented among the Canaanite gods, in the Ugaritic Texts and the writings of Sanchuniathon, both dated to the 2nd millennium BC (although Sanchuniathon's era is debated). In the Canaanite religion, Mot was the son of El (God), and the ruler of the "pit" called Mirey, where the dead resided.

3 Codex Vaticanus: para tô hadê meta tôn gêgenôn tous axonas autês (ΠΑΡΑ ΤΩ ΑΙΔΗ ΜΕΤΑ ΤΩΝ ΓΗΓΕΝΩΝ ΤΟΥΣΑΖΟΝΑΣΑΥΤΗΣ). Translation: near (or from, because,

near, besides) the Hades with the earth-born (or natives, aboriginals) of (or that, he, she, it, who, which, that) axis itself (or himself, herself)

- Aleppo Codex: ûål-rpåym môgltyh (**וְאֶל-רְפָאִים מַעְגְּלוֹתֶיהָ**).
Translation: and to Raphiam place of circles
- Leningrad Codex: ve'el-refa'im ma'geloteiha (וְאֶל-רְפָאִים מַעְגְּלֹתֶיהָ). Translation: and to Raphiam place of circles
- Targum to Proverbs: ûlegibārayā hilkātā dišbîlāhā (וּלְגִבָּרַיָּא הִלְכָתָא דִשְׁבִילָהָא). Translation: and the strong (or mighty) habitat (or law) of the path (or trail)

The Greek and Hebrew translations do not corroborate closely, and it appears that neither group of translators understood what they were translating. The term Refa'im (רְפָאִים), used in the Masoretic texts, is otherwise translated as Gigantes (Γίγαντεσ) in the Septuagint, indicating that the text the Greeks were working from did not use the term. The Greek term gêgenôn (γηγενων), referred to the 'earth-born,' and ancient race of hairy humans that supposedly lived on earth before the Titans made humanity. It was later used to refer to any aboriginal culture that was considered uncivilized.

The Greek term gêgenôn tous axonas (γηγενων τουσ αξονασ), appears to be a reference to the earth axis from Mesopotamian cosmology. In Neo-Assyrian cosmology, the earth axis was the theoretical axis of the universe, which ran from the highest place in the universe, known as Anshar (𒀭𒊹), to the lowest place in the universe, known as Kishar (𒆧𒊹). Anshar is generally translated as the "whole sky," however, also translates as the "limit of the sky." Likewise, Kishar translates as either the "whole earth," or the "limit of the Earth," and the axis was the theoretical line that connected them, around which the universe circled. The names are Neo-Assyrian, which suggests the phrase dates to a Neo-Assyrian Cuneiform translation made after Samaria was conquered by the Assyrians. The Hebrew translators must have read something similar in the Canaanite text they translated, but interpreted the "axis" as something rotational, and translated it as "place of the circles." As only the Hebrew translation clarifies that this is the god Mot, the phrase "the god" is in parentheses

Proverbs: Chapter 3

"Son, don't forget my laws but let your heart keep my words, as they will add to you through your length of existence, years of peaceful life. Don't let Mercy[1] and Faith[2] abandon you, but tie them around your neck, so will you find favor, and provide things honest in the sight of the Lord and men. Trust in God with all your heart, and do not revel in your own wisdom. In all your ways acquaint yourself with her, that she may rightly divide your paths. Do not be conceited in your own wisdom, but fear God, and leave from all evil. Then there will be health for your body and good keeping to your bones."

"Honor the Lord with your just labors, and give him the first of your fruits of righteousness, that your storehouses may be filled with grain, and that your presses may burst forth with wine. Son, don't hate the punishments of the Lord, or faint when you are rebuked by him, as whoever the Lord loves he rebukes, and punishes every son who he receives."

"Blessed is the man who has found Sophia, and the mortal who knows prudence. For it is better to trade for her than for treasures of gold and silver. She is more valuable than precious stones, no evil thing will resist her, and she is well known to all that approach her, and no precious thing is equal to her in value. For the length of existence and years of life are in her right hand, and in her left hand are wealth and glory, out of her mouth proceeds righteousness, and she carries law and mercy on her tongue. Her ways are good ways, and all her paths are peaceful. She is a tree of life to all that lay hold on her; and she is a secure help to all that trust themselves in her, as in the Lord."

"God through Sophia created the Earth, and through prudence, he prepared the heavens. By understanding the depths were broken up, and the clouds dropped water. Son, don't let them pass from you, but keep my counsel and understanding, that your mind may live, and that there may be grace round your neck, and it will be health to your flesh, and safety to your bones. That you may go confidently in peace in all your ways, and that your foot may not stumble. If you rest, you will be undismayed, and if you sleep, you will slumber sweetly. You will not be afraid of alarm coming on you, nor of approaching attacks of ungodly men. The Lord will be over all your ways and will establish your foot that you do not slip."

"Don't forget to do good to the poor whenever your hand may have the power to help him. Don't say, 'Come back another time, tomorrow, and I will give,' while you can do good for him, for you don't know what the next day will bring."

"Do not plan evil against your friend, living near you and trusting in you. Do not be ready to fight with a man without a cause, in case he harms you."

"Don't earn the reproaches of bad men, nor covet their ways. Every transgressor is unclean before the Lord, and he does not sit among the righteous."

"The curse of God is in the houses of the ungodly, but the homes of the just are blessed."

"The Lord resists the proud, but he gives grace to the humiliated."

"The wise will inherit glory, but the ungodly have exalted their own dishonor."

Proverbs: Chapter 3 Notes

1 Codex Vaticanus: eleêmosynae (ЄΛЄНМОСΥΝΑι). Translation: pity (or mercy, alms, charity)

• Aleppo Codex: hsd (חסד). Translation: loving-kindness (or benevolence, goodness)

• Leningrad Codex: hesed (חֶסֶד). Translation: loving-kindness (or benevolence, goodness)

• Targum to Proverbs: ṭêbûtā (טִיבוּתָא). Translation: goodness (or profit, pleasure)

2 Codex Vaticanus: pistis (ΠιСΤЄιС) Translation: faith (or creed, belief, Pistis)

- Aleppo Codex: åmt (אמת). Translation: truth (or correctness)
- Leningrad Codex: emet (אֱמֶת). Translation: truth (or correctness)
- Targum to Proverbs: qûšeṭā (קוּשְׁטָא). Translation: truth (or righteousness)

Proverbs: Chapter 4

Listen, children, to the instruction of a father, and pay attention in order to understand. I give you a great gift, don't forsake my law. I was also an obedient son to my father and loved by my mother, who spoke and instructed me, saying, "Let our words be fixed in your heart, keep our commandments, and don't forget them. Do not ignore the words from my mouth. Do not forget it, and it will cling to you. Love it, and it will keep you. Secure it, and it will exalt you. Honor it, so it may embrace you, so it may give to your head a crown of graces, and may cover you with a crown of delight."

"Listen, my son, and receive my words and the years of your life will be increased, so the resources of your life may be many. I teach you the ways of wisdom, and I cause you to follow along the correct paths. For when you go, your steps will not be straightened, and when you run, you will not be distressed. Take hold of my instructions and don't let go, but keep it for yourself for all your life. Don't go in the ways of the ungodly, nor covet the ways of transgressors. In whatever place they will pitch their camp, don't go there, but turn from them, and leave. For they can't sleep unless they have done evil, and their sleep is taken away, and they don't rest. For these live on the bread of ungodliness, and are drunken with the wine of transgression. But the ways of the righteous shine like the light, they go on and shine, until the day has fully come. The ways of the ungodly are dark, they don't know how they stumble."

"Son, listen to my voice, and apply your ear to my words, so that your fountains may not fail you, and keep them in your heart. They are life to those that find them and health to all their flesh. Keep your heart with the utmost care, for out of these are the issues of life. Don't have a quick mouth, and keep dishonesty away from your lips. Let your eyes look right on, and let your eyelids assent to just things. Make straight paths for your feet, and order your ways aright. Turn not aside to the right hand nor the left, but turn away your foot from an evil way, for God knows the ways on the right hand, but those on the left are crooked, and he will make your ways straight and will guide your steps in peace."

Proverbs: Chapter 5

"Son, listen to my wisdom, and apply your ear to my words, so you may have a good understanding, and so the discretion of my lips gives you an order. Pay no attention to a worthless woman, for honey drops from the lips of a prostitute, who for a season pleases your palate, but afterward, you will find her more bitter than gall, and sharper than a two-edged sword. For the feet of foolishness lead those who deal with her down to the grave with death, and her steps are not established. She does not follow the path of life, but her ways are slippery, and not easily known. Now then, my son, hear me, and don't disregard my words. Take yourself far away from her, and don't approach the doors of her house, in case you give away your life to others, and your substance to the merciless, and in case strangers become filled with your strength, and your labors come into the houses of strangers. You repent at last when the flesh of your body is consumed, and you will say, 'How have I hated instruction, and my heart avoided disapproval!'"

"I didn't hear the voice of he who instructed me and taught me, nor did I apply my ears. I was almost evil among the congregation and assembly. Drink water out of your own vessels and remove from your own springing wells. Don't let waters be spilled out of your fountain, but let your water go into your streets. Let them only be your own, and let no stranger partake with you. Let your fountain of water be truly your own, and rejoice with the wife of your youth. Let your loving heart and your graceful colt company with you, and let her be considered your own, and be with you at all times. Ravish her with love, and you will be greatly increased. Do not be intimate with a strange woman, nor fold yourself in the arms of a woman not your own. The ways of a man are before the eyes of God, and he looks on all his paths. Iniquities trap a man, and everyone is bound in the chains of his own sins. Such a man dies with the uninstructed, and he is thrown out from the abundance of his own substance and has perished through foolishness."

Proverbs: Chapter 6

"Son, if you become responsible for your friend, you will deliver your hand to an enemy. For a man's own lips become a strong snare to him, and he is caught with the lips of his own mouth. Son, do what I command you, and deliver yourself, for on your friend's account you will come into the power of evil men. Do not rest, but stir up also your friend for whom you have become responsible. Do not let sleep enter your eyes, or slumber enter your eyelids, so you can save yourself like a doe out of trouble, and like a bird out of a snare."

"Consider the ant, you sluggard, and observe and copy his ways, and become wiser than he is. He has no owner, or anyone to compel him, and is under no master, yet he prepares food for himself in the summer and lays by an abundant store in the harvest. Or consider the bee, and learn how diligent she is, and how earnestly she is engaged in her work, whose labors kings and private men use for health, and she is desired and respected by all, though weak in body, she is advanced by honoring wisdom. How long will you lie, sluggard? When will you awake out of sleep? You sleep a little, and you rest a little, and you slumber a short time, and you fold your arms over your chest a little. Then poverty comes on you like an evil traveler, and poverty as a swift courier, but if you are diligent, your harvest will arrive like a fountain, and poverty will flee away as a bad courier."

"A foolish man and a transgressor go along paths that are not good. The same winks with the eye, makes a sign with his foot and teaches with the beckoning of his fingers. His perverse heart devises evils, at all times one like this causes troubles to a city. Therefore his destruction will come suddenly, overthrown and irretrievably ruined. He rejoices in all things which God hates, and he is ruined because of impurity of mind. The eye of the haughty, a tongue unjust, hands shedding the blood of the just, a heart devising evil thoughts, and feet rushing to do evil, are hateful to God. An unjust witness kindles falsehoods, and brings on quarrels between brothers."

"Son, keep the laws of your father, and don't reject the ordinances of your mother, but bind them on your mind[1] eternally, and hang them like a chain around your neck. Whenever you walk, lead this along and let it be with you, that it may talk with you when you wake. For the commandment of the law is a lamp and a light, a way of life, reproof also and correction, to keep you continually from a married woman, and from the defamation of a strange tongue. Don't let the desire for beauty overcome you, nor be caught by your eyes or be captivated by her eyelids. For the value of a prostitute is as much as of one loaf, and a woman hunts for the precious minds of men."

"Will anyone bind fire in his bosom, and not burn his garments? Will anyone walk on burning coals, and not burn his feet? Likewise is he who goes into a married woman. He will not be held guiltless, nor anyone that touches her. It is not to be considered if one should be stolen, for he who steals when hungry may satisfy his mind, but if he should be caught, he will repay seven times and will deliver himself by giving all his goods. The adulterer through lack of sense procures destruction to his mind. He endures both pain and disgrace, and his reproach will never be erased. For the mind of her husband is full of jealousy, and he will not spare in the day of vengeance. He will not forego his enmity for any ransom, nor will he be reconciled for many gifts."

Proverbs: Chapter 6 Notes

1 Codex Vaticanus: psychên (ΤΥΧΗΝ). Translation: mind (or personality, psyche)

- Aleppo Codex: lbk (לבך). Translation: heart
- Leningrad Codex: libbecha (לִבְךָ). Translation: heart
- Targum to Proverbs: libbāk (לִבָּךְ). Translation: heart (or mind)

Proverbs: Chapter 7

"Son, follow my words and hide with you my commandments. Son, honor the Lord, and you will be strong. Fear none but him. Keep my commandments, and you will live, and keep my words as the pupils of your eyes. Bind them on your fingers, and write them on the table of your heart. Say that wisdom is your sister, and gain prudence as an acquaintance for yourself. That she may keep you from the strange and wicked woman if she should assail you with flattering words. She looks from a window out of her house into the streets, at one whom she may see of the senseless ones, a young man void of understanding, passing by the corner in the passages near her house, and speaking, in the dark of the evening, when there happens to be the stillness of the night and darkness, and the woman meets him having the appearance of a prostitute, that causes the hearts of young men to flutter. She is fickle and debauched, and her feet will not stay at home."

"At one time she wanders around outside, yet at another time she lies in wait in the streets, at every corner. Then she caught him and kissed him, and with an impudent face said to him, I have a peace offering today and I pay my vows, therefore I came out to meet you, desiring your face, and I have found you. I have spread my bed with sheets, and I have covered it with a double tapestry from Egypt. I have sprinkled my couch with saffron, and my house with cinnamon. Come, and let us enjoy love until the morning. Come, and let us embrace in love. My husband is not at home but is gone on a long journey, having taken in his hand a bundle of money, and after many days he will return to his house. So with much conversation, she prevailed on him to go astray, and with the snares of her lips forced him from the right path."

"He followed her, being gently led on, like an ox is led to the slaughter, and like a dog to chains, or like a deer shot in the liver with an arrow. He rushes like a bird into a snare not knowing that he is running for his life. Now then, my son, listen to me and attend to the words of my mouth. don't let your heart turn aside to her ways: for she has wounded and cast down many, and those whom she has slain are innumerable. Her house is the way of Sheol, leading down to the chambers of Mot."

Proverbs: Chapter 8

You will proclaim wisdom, that understanding may be obedient to you. For she is on lofty eminences and stands among the ways. For she sits by the gates of princes, and sings in the entrances, saying, "You, men I praise and speak my voice to the sons of men. You are simple, understand subtlety, and you who are untaught, imbibe knowledge. Listen to me, for I will speak solemn truths, and will produce right sayings from my lips. My throat will meditate on truth, and false lips are an abomination before me. All the words of my mouth are in righteousness, and there is nothing in them that is wrong or perverse. They are all evident to those that understand, and right to those that find knowledge. Receive instruction and not silver, and knowledge rather than pure gold. Wisdom is better than precious gems, and no valuable substance is of equal worth with it. I, Sophia, have lived with counsel and knowledge, and I have called on understanding."

"The fear of the Lord hates unrighteousness, and insolence, and pride, and the ways of wicked men, and I hate the perverse ways of bad men. Counsel and safety are mine, prudence is mine, and strength is mine. By me kings reign, and princes decree justice. By me nobles become great, and monarchs by me rule over the earth. I love those that love me, and they who seek me will find me. Wealth and glory belong to me, yes, abundant possessions and righteousness. It is better to have my fruit than to have gold and precious stones, and my produce is better than pure silver. I walk in ways of righteousness, and am conversant with the paths of judgment, and that I may divide substance to them that love me, and may fill their treasures with good things. If I state to you the things that happen daily, I will also remember to tell the things of old."

"The Lord made me first among his works. He created me before there was time, in the beginning, before he made the Earth, even before he made Tiamat,[1] before the fountains of water came up, before the mountains were lifted, and before all hills, he created me."

"The Lord made countries and uninhabited tracks, and the highest inhabited parts of the world. When he prepared the sky, I was present with him, and when he prepared his throne on the winds, and when he strengthened the clouds above, and when he secured the fountains of the Earth. When he strengthened the foundations of the Earth, I was by him, suiting myself to him, I was that which he took delight in, and I rejoiced daily in his presence continually. He rejoiced when he had completed the world, and rejoiced among the children of men. Now then, my son, hear me, blessed is the man who will listen to me and the mortal who will keep my ways. Hear wisdom and be wise, and do not be strangers to it. Watch daily at my doors, and wait at the posts of my entrances. My outgoings are the outgoings of life, and in them is prepared favor from the Lord. But they who sin against me act wickedly against their own minds, and they who hate me love death."

Proverbs: Chapter 8 Notes

1 Codex Vaticanus: abyssous (ᴀʙʏccoc). Translation: abyss (or deep chasms, depths)

- Aleppo Codex: thmût (תהמות)

- Leningrad Codex: tehomot (תְהֹמֹות)

- Targum to Proverbs: tehômê (תְהֹומֵי). Translation: abyssmal (or unfathomable)

The word found in the Masoretic text, is a feminine form of tehôm (תְהֹום), meaning "depths." This word was the name of the ancient Semitic goddess of the depths, water, and creation, recorded as Tiamat (𒀭𒁲𒈠) in Akkadian Cuneiform, and Thmt (𐎚𐎅𐎎𐎚) in Ugaritic Canaanite. She was widely worshiped during the Bronze Age, but disappeared from Canaanite religion in the early Iron Age, indicating this proverb dates to that era.

In Mesopotamia, the goddess became less important in the Iron Age but was still revered as one of the ancient creator deities. When the Greeks ruled Mesopotamia, they translated her name as Thalattê (Θαλάττη), which means the translators at the Library of Alexandria were working from a text that did not include her name, and read thǔmǎ (ΝϞϽ)Ϟ), meaning depths instead of Thmůt (Ϝϟ)Ͻ)Ϟ), meaning Tiamat. As the Hebrew translators would not have added an ancient goddess to the Aramaic text they translated, it suggests that not all of Proverbs was translated into Hebrew from Aramaic, and some verses might have been retained in the older Canaanite (Judahite, Samaritan, or Edomite) text. So far, no Phoenician fragments of Proverbs have been found among the Dead Sea Scrolls, however, only two fragments of Proverbs have been found among the Dead Sea Scrolls, suggesting it was not a popular text.

Proverbs: Chapter 9

Sophia has built a house for herself and set up seven pillars. She has killed her beasts, and she has prepared her wine in a bowl and prepared her table. She has sent out her servants, calling with a loud proclamation to the feast, saying, "Whoever is foolish, let him turn aside to me," and to those that lack understanding she says, "Come, eat of my bread, and drink wine which I have prepared for you. Leave foolishness, that you may reign forever, and seek wisdom, and improve understanding by knowledge."

"He who reproves evil men will dishonor himself, and he who insults an ungodly man will disgrace himself. Do not rebuke evil men, in case they should hate you. Rebuke a wise man, and he will love you. Allow a wise man, and he will be wiser. Instruct a just man, and he will receive more instruction. The fear of the Lord is the peak of wisdom, and the counsel of saints[1] is understanding, as knowing the law is the character of a sound mind. In this way, you will live long, and years of your life will be added to you."

"Son, if you are wise for yourself, you will also be wise for your neighbors, and if you should prove wicked, you alone will carry the evil. He who follows falsehoods and attempts to rule the winds will follow birds in their flight, for he has forgotten the ways of his own vineyard, and he has caused the axles of his own husbandry to go astray. He goes through a dry desert, and a land appointed to drought, and he gathers barrenness with his hands. A foolish and bold woman, who knows no modesty, comes to lack food. She sits at the doors of her house, on a seat openly in the streets, calling to passers-by, and to those that are going right on their ways, saying, 'Whoever is most senseless of you, let him turn aside to me,' and I exhort those that lack prudence, saying, 'Take and enjoy secret bread and the sweet water of theft.' But he knows that mighty men die by her, and he falls in with a snare of Sheol. Hurry away, don't remain in the place, nor look at her or else you will go for strange water. Instead, abstain from strange water, and don't drink from a strange fountain, so you may live long, and years of life may be added to you."

Proverbs: Chapter 9 Notes

1 Codex Vaticanus: agiôn (ܐܓܝܘܢ). Translation: saints

• Aleppo Codex: qdšym (קְדֹשִׁים). Translation: sacred (plural form)

• Leningrad Codex: kedoshim (קְדֹשִׁים). Translation: sacred (plural form)

• Targum on Proverbs: qadîšê (קַדִּישֵׁי). Translation: holies (masculine form)

Proverbs: Chapter 10

A wise son makes his father glad, but a foolish son is a grief to his mother.

Treasures will not profit the lawless, but righteousness will deliver from death.

The Lord will not starve a righteous mind, but he will overthrow the life of the ungodly.

Poverty brings a man low, but the hands of the vigorous make rich.

A son who is instructed will be wise and will use the fool for a servant.

A wise son is saved from heat, but a lawless son is the blighted winds in the harvest.

The blessing of the Lord is on the head of the just, but untimely grief will cover the mouth of the ungodly.

The memory of the just is praised, but the name of the ungodly man is extinguished.

A wise man in heart will receive commandments, but he who is unguarded in his lips will be overthrown in his perverseness.

He who walks simply walks confidently, but he who perverts his ways will be known.

He who winks with his eyes deceitfully procures griefs for men, but he who reproves boldly is a peace-maker.

There is a fountain of life in the hand of a righteous man, but destruction will cover the mouth of the ungodly.

Hatred stirs up strife, but affection covers all that do not love strife.

He who brings wisdom from his lips defeats the fool with a stick.

The wise will hide discretion, but the mouth of the hasty draws near to ruin.

The wealth of rich men is a strong city, but poverty is the ruin of the ungodly.

The works of the righteous produce life, but the fruits of the ungodly produce sins.

Instruction keeps the right ways of life, but poor instruction leads astray.

Righteous lips cover enmity, but they who speak insults are most foolish.

By a multitude of words, you will not escape sin, but if you refrain your lips you will be prudent.

The tongue of the just is tried silver, but the heart of the ungodly will fail.

The lips of the righteous know sublime truths, but the foolish die in poverty.

The blessing of the Lord is on the head of the righteous, it enriches him, and heartbreak will not be added to it.

A fool does laughter in sports, but wisdom brings out prudence for a man.

The ungodly are engulfed in destruction, but the desire of the righteous is acceptable.

When the storm passes by, the ungodly vanishes away, but the righteous turns aside and escapes forever.

As a sour grape is hurtful to the teeth, and smoke to the eyes, so iniquity hurts those that practice it.

The fear of the Lord adds to the length of days, but the years of the ungodly will be shortened.

Joy rests along with the righteous, but the hope of the ungodly will perish.

The fear of the Lord is a stronghold of the saints, but ruin comes to those who work wickedness.

The righteous will never fail, but the ungodly will not live on the earth.

The mouth of the righteous drops wisdom, but the tongue of the unjust will perish.

The lips of just men drop grace, but the mouth of the ungodly is perverse.

Proverbs: Chapter 11

False balances are an abomination before the Lord, but a just weight is acceptable to him.

Wherever pride enters, there will also be disgrace, but the mouth of the lowly meditates wisdom.

When a just man dies he leaves regret, but the destruction of the ungodly is speedy and causes joy.

Possessions will not profit in a day of anger, but righteousness will deliver from death.

Righteousness traces out blameless paths, but ungodliness encounters unjust dealing.

The righteousness of upright men delivers them, but transgressors are caught in their own destruction.

At the death of a just man his hope does not perish, but the boast of the ungodly perishes.

A righteous man escapes from a snare, and the ungodly man is delivered up in his place.

In the mouth of ungodly men is a snare to citizens, but the understanding of righteous men is prosperous.

In the prosperity of righteous men, a city prospers, but by the mouth of ungodly men, it is overthrown.

At the blessing of the upright, a city will be exalted.

A man void of understanding sneers at his fellow citizens, but a sensible man is quiet.

A double-tongued man discloses the secret counsels of an assembly, but he who is faithful in spirit conceals matters.

Those who have no guidance fall like leaves, but in much counsel there is safety.

A bad man does harm wherever he meets a just man, and he hates the sound of safety.

A gracious wife brings glory to her husband, but a woman hating righteousness is a theme of dishonor.

The slothful come to lack, but the diligent support themselves with wealth.

A merciful man does good to his own mind, but the merciless destroys his own body.

An ungodly man performs unrighteous works, but the seed of the righteous is a reward of truth.

A righteous son is born for life, but the persecution of the ungodly ends in death.

Perverse ways are an abomination to the Lord, but all those who are blameless in their ways are acceptable to him.

He who unjustly strikes hands will not be unpunished, but he who sows righteousness will receive a faithful reward.

As an ornament in a swine's snout, so is beauty to an ill-minded woman.

All the desire of the righteous is good, but the hope of the ungodly will perish.

Some scatter their own and make it more, and there are some also who gather, yet have less.

Every sincere mind is blessed, but a passionate man is not graceful.

May he who hoards grain leave it to the nation, but a blessing is on the head of him that gives it.

He who devises good counsels seeks good favor, but as for he who searches for evil, evil will catch him.

He who trusts in wealth will fall, but he who helps righteous men will rise.

He who does not deal graciously with his own house will inherit the wind, and the fool will be a servant to the wise man.

Out of the fruit of righteousness grows a tree of life, but the minds of transgressors are cut off before their time.

If the righteous scarcely be saved, where will the ungodly and the sinner appear?

Proverbs: Chapter 12

He who loves instruction loves sense, but he who hates disapproval is a fool.

He who has found favor with the Lord is made better, but a transgressor will be passed over in silence.

A man will not prosper by wickedness, but the roots of the righteous will not be taken up.

A virtuous woman is a crown to her husband, but a bad woman destroys her husband like a worm in wood.

The thoughts of the righteous are true judgments, but ungodly men devise deceits.

The words of ungodly men are crafty, but the mouth of the upright will deliver them.

When the ungodly is overthrown, he vanishes away, but the houses of the just remain.

The mouth of an understanding man is praised by a man, but he who is dull of heart is held in derision.

Better is a dishonored man serving himself than one honoring himself but lacking bread.

A righteous man pities the lives of his livestock, but the bowels of the ungodly are unmerciful.

He who tills his own land will be satisfied with bread, but they who pursue vanities are void of understanding.

He who enjoys himself in banquets of wine will leave dishonor in his own strongholds.

The desires of the ungodly are evil, but the roots of the godly are firmly set.

For the sin of his lips, a sinner falls into a snare, but a righteous man escapes from them.

He whose looks are gentle will be pitied, but he who fights at the gates will afflict minds.

The mind of a man will be filled with good from the fruits of his mouth, and the recompense of his lips will be given to him.

The ways of fools are right in their own eyes, but a wise man listens to counsels.

A fool declares his anger the same day, but a prudent man hides his own disgrace.

A righteous man declares the open truth, but an unjust witness is deceitful.

Some wound as they speak like swords, but the tongues of the wise heal.

True lips establish testimony, but a hasty witness has an unjust tongue.

There is deceit in the heart of he that imagines evil, but they who love peace will rejoice.

No injustice will please a just man, but the ungodly will be filled with mischief.

Lying lips are an abomination to the Lord, but he who deals faithfully is accepted by him.

An understanding man is a throne of wisdom, but the heart of fools will meet with curses.

The hand of chosen men will easily obtain rule, but the deceitful will be prey.

A terrible word troubles the heart of a righteous man, but a good message caused him to celebrate.

A just arbitrator will be his own friend, but mischief will pursue sinners, and the way of ungodly men will lead them astray.

A deceitful man will catch no game, but a blameless man is a precious possession.

In the ways of righteousness is life, but the ways of those who remember injuries lead to death.

Proverbs: Chapter 13

A wise son is obedient to his father, but a disobedient son will be destroyed.

A good man will eat of the fruits of righteousness, but the lives of transgressors will perish before their time.

He who keeps his own mouth keeps his own life, but he who is hasty with his lips will bring terror on himself.

Every slothful man desires, but the hands of the active are diligent.

A righteous man hates an unjust word, but an ungodly man is ashamed and has no confidence.

There are some who, having nothing, enrich themselves, and there are some who bring themselves down from much wealth.

A man's own wealth is the ransom of his life, but the poor endure no threats.

The righteous always have light, but the light of the ungodly is quenched.

Sneaky minds go astray in sins, but honest men pity and are merciful.

A bad man does evil with insolence, but they who are judges of themselves are wise.

Wealth taken hastily with iniquity is diminished, but he who gathers for himself with godliness will be increased.

The righteous is merciful and lends.

Better is he who begins to help honestly than he who promises and leads another to hope, for a good desire is a tree of life.

He who slights a matter will be slighted of it, but he who fears the commandment has a healthy mind.

To a crafty son, there will be nothing good, but a wise servant undertakes prosperous actions, and his way will be directed correctly.

The law of the wise is a fountain of life, but the man void of understanding will die by a snare.

Sound discretion gives favor, and to know the law is part of a sound understanding, but the ways of scorners lead to destruction.

Every prudent man acts with knowledge, but the fool displays his own mischief.

A rash king will fall into mischief, but a wise messenger will deliver him.

Instruction removes poverty and disgrace, but he who attends to disapproval will be honored.

The desires of the godly gladden the mind, but the works of the ungodly are far from knowledge.

If you walk with wise men you will be wise, but he who walks with fools will be known.

Evil will pursue sinners, but goodwill overtakes the righteous.

A good man will inherit children's children, and the wealth of ungodly men is laid up for the just.

The righteous will spend many years in wealth, but the unrighteous will perish suddenly.

He who spares the wand hates his son, but he who loves carefully teaches him.

A just man eats and satisfies his mind, but the minds of the ungodly are lacking.

Proverbs: Chapter 14

Wise women build houses, but a foolish one pulls hers down with her hands.

He who walks uprightly fears the Lord, but he who is perverse in his ways will be dishonored.

Out of the mouth of fools comes a wand of pride, but the lips of the wise preserve them.

Where no oxen are, the cribs are clean, but where there is abundant produce, the strength of the ox is apparent.

A faithful witness does not lie, but an unjust witness kindles falsehoods.

You will seek wisdom with bad men, and will not find it, but discretion is easily available with the prudent.

All things are adverse to a foolish man, but wise lips are the weapons of discretion.

The wisdom of the prudent will understand their ways, but the foolishness of fools leads them astray.

The houses of transgressors will need purification, but the houses of the just are acceptable.

If a man's mind is intelligent, his mind is sorrowful, and when he rejoices, he has no fellowship with pride.

The houses of ungodly men will be destroyed, but the tents of those who walk uprightly will stand.

There is a way which seems to be right with men, but the ends of it reach to the depths of Sheol.

Grief does not mingle with mirth and joy, and in the end, comes grief.

A strong-hearted man will be filled with his own ways and a good man with his own thoughts.

The simple believes every word, but the prudent man thinks more deeply.

A wise man fears and departs from evil, but the fool trusts in himself and joins himself with the transgressor.

A passionate man acts inconsiderately, but a sensible man bears up under many things.

Fools have mischief for their portion, but the prudent will take fast hold of understanding.

Evil men will fall before the good, and the ungodly will attend at the gates of the righteous.

Friends will hate poor friends, but the friends of the rich are many.

He who dishonors the destitute sins, but he who pities the poor is most blessed.

They that go astray devise evils, but the good devise mercy and truth.

The framers of evil do not understand mercy and truth, but compassion and faithfulness are with the framers of good.

With everyone careful, there is abundance, but the pleasure-taking and indolent will be in lack.

A prudent man is the crown of the wise, but the occupation of fools is evil.

A faithful witness will deliver a mind from evil, but a deceitful man kindles falsehoods.

In the fear of the Lord is great confidence, and he provides his children strength.

The commandment of the Lord is a fountain of life, and it causes men to turn aside from the snare of death.

In a populous nation is the glory of a king, but in the failure of people is the ruin of a prince.

A man slow to anger abounds in wisdom, but a man of impatient spirit is very foolish.

A meek-spirited man is a healer of the heart, but a sensitive heart is a corruption of the bones.

He who slanders and exaggerates is like a poison, but he who honors him pities the poor.

The ungodly will be driven away in his wickedness, but he who is secure in his own holiness is just.

There is wisdom in the good heart of a man, but in the heart of fools, it is not discerned.

Righteousness exalts a nation and lacking[1] it, a people error.

An understanding servant is acceptable to a king, and by his good behavior, he removes disgrace.

Proverbs: Chapter 14 Notes

1 Codex Vaticanus: elassonousi (ЄΛΛϹϹΟΝΟΥϹΙ). Translation: deficient

• Dead Sea Scroll 4QProv[b]: hsr (חסר). Translation: absent (or missing, deficient)

• Aleppo Codex: hsd (חסד). Translation: loving-kindness (or benevolence, goodness)

• Leningrad Codex: hesed (חֶסֶד). Translation: loving-kindness (or benevolence, goodness)

• Targum on Proverbs: hisdā (חִסְדָא). Translation: shame (or revilement)

This is one of the few places where the Masoretic texts differ from the Septuagint, Dead Sea Scrolls, and Targum on Proverbs. In this case, it appears that both the Leningrad Codex and Aleppo Codex descend from a copy of Proverbs where a scribe had copied an R (ר) as a D (ד), fundamentally changing the meaning of the verse. As the error had to have taken place after both the Greek and Hebrew translations of Proverbs were made, but before the Masoretes began copying the text, it must have taken place in the first 300 years of the Christian Era. Given that only two fragments of Proverbs have been found among the Dead Sea Scrolls, it appears to have been an unpopular text among Jews in the early Christian era, and the Masoretes probably did not have access to multiple copies for comparison. The Greek translation of Proverbs was popular among Gnostics at the time, which suggests the unpopularity among Jews was due to differences regarding the nature of Sophia (Wisdom), who was treated as equal to the Lord in Proverbs and claimed to be the first creation of God. Most Gnostics viewed Sophia as the wife of God, which was inconsistent with the teachings of the Pharisees and Sadducees at the time.

Proverbs: Chapter 15

Anger slays even wise men, yet a submissive answer turns away anger, but a terrible word stirs up anger.

The tongue of the wise knows what is good, but the mouth of the foolish tells out evil things.

The eyes of the Lord see both the evil and the good in every place.

The wholesome tongue is a tree of life, and he who keeps it will be filled with understanding.

A fool scorns his father's instruction, but he who keeps his commandments is more prudent.

In abounding righteousness is a great strength, but the ungodly will completely perish from the Earth.

In the houses of the righteous is much strength, but the fruits of the ungodly will perish.

The lips of the wise are bound by discretion, but the hearts of the foolish are not safe.

The sacrifices of the ungodly are an abomination to the Lord, but the prayers of those who walk honestly are acceptable to him.

The ways of an ungodly man are an abomination to the Lord, but he loves those who follow after righteousness.

The instruction of the simple is known by them that pass by, but they who hate disapproval die disgracefully.

Sheol and destruction are manifest to the Lord, how will the hearts of men not also be?

An uninstructed person will not love those who reprove him, neither will he associate with the wise.

When the heart rejoices the countenance is cheerful, but when it is in sorrow, the countenance is sad.

An upright heart seeks discretion, but the mouth of the uninstructed will experience evils.

The eyes of the wicked are always looking for evil things, but the good are always quiet.

Better is a small portion with the fear of the Lord, than great treasures without the fear of the Lord.

Better is an entertainment of plants with friendliness and kindness than a feast of calves, with enmity.

A passionate man stirs up strife, but he who is slow to anger appeases even a rising one.

A man slow to anger will extinguish quarrels, but an ungodly man rather stirs them up.

The ways of sluggards are strewn with thorns, but those of the diligent are made smooth.

A wise son gladdens his father, but a foolish son sneers at his mother.

The ways of a foolish man are void of sense, but a wise man proceeds on his way correctly.

Those who don't honor council, put off deliberation, but counsel lives in the hearts of counselors.

A bad man will not listen to counsel, nor will he say anything sensible, or good for the common good.

The thoughts of the wise are ways of life, that he may turn aside and escape from Sheol.

The Lord pulls down the houses of scorners, but he establishes the borders of the widow.

An unrighteous thought is an abomination to the Lord, but the sayings of the pure are held in honor.

A receiver of bribes destroys himself, but he who hates the receiving of bribes is safe.

By alms and by faithful dealings sins are purged away, but by the fear of the Lord, everyone departs from evil.

The hearts of the righteous meditate on faithfulness, but the mouth of the ungodly answers evil things.

The ways of righteous men are acceptable to the Lord, and through them even enemies become friends.

God is far from the ungodly, but he listens to the prayers of the righteous.

Better are small receipts with righteousness, than abundant fruits with unrighteousness.

Let the heart of a man think justly, that his steps may be rightly ordered by God.

The eye that sees rightly rejoices the heart, and a good report fattens the bones.

He who rejects instruction hates himself, but he who remembers disapproval loves his mind.

The fear of the Lord is instruction and wisdom, and the highest honor will correspond with it.

Proverbs: Chapter 16

All the works of the humiliated man are manifest with God, but the ungodly will perish in an evil day.

Everyone proud in heart is unclean before God, and he who unjustly strikes hands with hand will not be held guiltless.

He who rejects instruction hates himself, but he who learns from punishment loves his mind.

The fear of the Lord is instruction and wisdom and will result in the highest honor.

The beginning of a good way is to do justly, and it is more acceptable to God than to offer sacrifices.

He who seeks the Lord will find knowledge with righteousness, and they who rightly seek him will find peace.

All of the works of the Lord are righteousness, and the ungodly are kept for the evil day.

There is an oracle on the lips of a king, and his mouth will not error in judgment.

The poise of the balance is righteousness with the Lord, and his works are righteous measures.

A transgressor is an abomination to a king, as the throne of rule is established through righteousness.

Righteous lips are acceptable to a king, and he loves the right words.

The anger of a king is a messenger of death, but a wise man will pacify him.

The son of a king is in the light of life, and they who are in favor with him, are like a cloud of rain.

The land of wisdom is more valuable than gold, and the brood of prudence is more valuable than silver.

The paths of life turn aside from evil, and the ways of righteousness are the length of life.

He who receives instruction will be in prosperity, and he who regards disapproval will be made wise.

He who keeps his ways preserves his own mind, and he who loves his life will spare his mouth.

Pride goes before destruction, and foolishness before a fall.

Better is a meek-spirited man with lowliness, than one who divides spoils with the proud.

He who is skillful in business finds good, but he who trusts in God is more blessed.

Men call the wise and understanding evil, but they who are pleasing in speech will hear more.

Understanding is a fountain of life to its possessors, but the instruction of fools is evil.

The heart of the wise will discern the things which proceed from his own mouth, and on his lips, he will wear knowledge.

Good words are honeycombs, the sweetness is a healing of the mind.

Some ways seem to be right to a man, but the end of them looks to the depth of Sheol.

A man who labors, labors for himself, and drives ruin from himself.

The perverse bears destruction on his own mouth, a foolish man digs up evil for himself, and treasures fire on his own lips.

A perverse man spreads mischief and will kindle a torch of deceit with injuries, and he separates friends.

A transgressor tries to ensnare friends and leads them in ways that are not good.

The man that fixes his eyes devises perverse things and marks out with his lips all evil, he is a furnace of wickedness.

Old age is a crown of honor, but it is found in the ways of righteousness.

A man slow to anger is better than a strong man, and he who governs his temper better than he who takes a city.

All that comes to the ungodly comes from their hearts, but all righteous things are from the Lord.

Proverbs: Chapter 17

Better is a meal with pleasure in peace than a house full of many good things and unjust sacrifices, with struggle.

A wise servant has rule over foolish masters and will divide portions among his brothers.

As silver and gold are tried in a furnace, so are choice hearts with the Lord.

A bad man listens to the tongue of transgressors, but a righteous man ignores lips.

He who laughs at the poor provokes him that made him, and he who rejoices at the destruction of another will not be held guiltless, but he who has compassion will find mercy.

Children's children are the crown of old men, and their fathers are the glory of children.

The faithful have the whole world full of wealth, but the faithless, not even a gerah.[1]

Faithful lips will not suit a fool, or lying lips a just man.

Instruction is for those who use it as a gracious reward, and wherever it may turn, it will prosper.

He who conceals injuries seeks love, but he who hates to hide them separates friends and families.

A threat breaks down the heart of a wise man, but a fool, when scourged does not understand.

Every bad man stirs up strife, but the Lord will send out against him an unmerciful messenger.

Care may befall a man of understanding, but fools will meditate evils.

Whoever rewards evil for good, evil will not be removed from his house.

The rightful rule gives power to words, but sedition and strife precede poverty.

He who pronounces the unjust as just, and the just as unjust, is unclean and abominable with God.

Why does the fool have wealth? A senseless man will not be able to purchase wisdom.

He who exalts his own house seeks ruin, and he who turns aside from instruction will fall into mischief.

Do you have a friend for every time? Let brothers be useful in times of distress, as this is the reason they are born.

A foolish man applauds and rejoices over himself. If he became responsible, he would make himself responsible for his own friends.

A lover of sin rejoices in strife, and the hard-hearted man does no good.

A man of a deceitful tongue will fall into injuries, and the heart of a fool is grief to its possessor.

A father does not rejoice over an uneducated son, but a wise son brings joy to his mother.

A glad heart promotes health, but the bones of a sorrowful man dry up.

The ways of a man who unjustly receives gifts in his chest do not prosper, and an ungodly man perverts the ways of righteousness.

The countenance of a wise man is sensible, but the eyes of a fool go to the edges of the Earth.

A foolish son is a cause of anger to his father and grief to her that carried him.

It is not right to punish a righteous man, nor is it holy to plot against righteous princes.

He who chooses not to speak a hard word is discreet, and a patient man is wise.

Wisdom will be imputed to a fool who asks after wisdom, and he who holds his peace will seem to be sensible.

Proverbs: Chapter 17 Notes

1 Codex Vaticanus: obolos (ΟΒΟΛΟC)

• The Masoretic texts does not include this verse.

• The Targum to Proverbs does not include this verse.

The obol was a Greek coin used from around 1100 BC, worth ⅙ of a drachma, approximately 0.72 grams of silver. In the other books of the Septuagint where the term obol is used, the term found in the Leningrad Codex is gerah (גֵּרָה), which was worth one-twentieth of a shekel. As the obol was not used in ancient Canaan or Samaria, the translation of gerah is used, as that is almost certainly what the Greeks translated as obol.

Proverbs: Chapter 18

A man who wishes to separate from friends makes excuses, but at all times he will be liable to reproach.

A senseless man feels no need for wisdom, as he is instead led by foolishness.

When an ungodly man comes into a depth of evils, he despises them, but dishonor and reproach come on him.

A word in the heart of a man is deep well, and a river and fountain of life spring forth.

It is not good to accept the person of the ungodly, nor is it holy to pervert justice in judgment.

The lips of a fool bring him into trouble, and his bold mouth calls for death.

A fool's mouth is ruined to him, and his lips are a snare to his mind.

Fear throws down the slothful and the minds of the hermaphrodite[1] will hunger.

A man who doesn't help himself through his labor is a brother to he who ruins himself.

The name of the Lord is of great strength, and the righteous running to it are exalted.

The wealth of a rich man is a strong city, and its glory throws a broad shadow.

Before ruin a man's heart is exalted, and before honor, it is humiliated.

Whoever answers a word before he hears the question, is foolish and there will be a reproach on him.

A wise servant calms a man's anger; but who can endure a faint-hearted man?

The heart of the sensible man purchases discretion and the ears of the wise seek understanding.

A man's gift enlarges him and seats him among princes.

A righteous man accuses himself at the beginning of his speech, but when he has entered the attack, the adversary is reproved.

A silent man quells strife and determines between great powers.

A brother helped by a brother is a strong and high city and is as strong as a well-founded palace.

A man fills his belly with the fruits of his mouth, and he will be satisfied with the fruits of his lips.

Life and death are in the power of the tongue, and they who control it will eat the fruits of it.

He who has found a good wife has found favor and has received joy from God.

He who divorces a good wife divorces a good thing, and he who keeps an adulteress is foolish and ungodly.

He who divorces a good wife divorces a good thing, and he who keeps an adulteress is foolish and ungodly.

Proverbs: Chapter 18 Notes

1 Codex Vaticanus: androgynôn (ᴀɴᴅᴘᴏᴦᴙɴᴡɴ) the plural form of andrógyno (ανδρόγυνο) Translation: married couple, "man and woman." Generally, in this context, it is accepted as a variant of andrógynos (ανδρόγυνος) meaning hermaphrodite, which shows up later in Proverbs.

The Aleppo Codex has a different sentence: âḥ ḥûå lbôl mšḥyt (אח הוא לבעל משחית) which translates approximately as "is a brother to him that is lord of destruction." The difference between the Hebrew and Greek texts has been a matter of great debate for over a millennium. Latin and other Western European translations, use terms meaning "effeminate" instead of hermaphrodite, however, the Greek term androgynôn (ανδρόγυνος) is specific. It is theorized by modern scholars that this text was inserted into Proverbs by the translators at the Library of Alexandria as a response or rebuttal of Plato's Banquet, which claimed that the human species originally had three equal genders: male, female, and hermaphrodite (ανδρόγυνος). In this context, the term hermaphrodite meant a dual-gendered human and not an intersex human which was known as hermaphrodite in Greco-Roman civilization. Early Christians interpreted this reference to the hermaphrodites as evidence that Plato had studied the Hebrew scriptures, however, modern scholars view it the opposite way as the reference is not found in the Masoretic text.

Proverbs: Chapter 19

The foolishness of a man spoils his ways, and he blames God in his heart.

Wealth acquires many friends, but the poor is deserted even of the friends he has.

A false witness will not be unpunished, and he who accuses unjustly will not escape.

Many court the favor of kings, but every bad man becomes a reproach to another man.

Everyone who hates his poor brother will also be far from friendship.

A good understanding will draw near to them that know it, and a sensible man will find it.

He who does much harm perfects mischief, and he who uses provoking words will not escape.

He who procures wisdom loves himself, and he who keeps wisdom will find good.

A false witness will not be unpunished, and whoever will kindle mischief will perish by it.

Delight does not suit a fool, nor is it seemly if a servant should begin to rule with haughtiness.

A merciful man is patient, and his triumph overtakes transgressors.

The threatening of a king is like the roaring of a lion, but as dew on the grass, so is his favor.

A foolish son is a disgrace to his father, vows paid out of the hire of a prostitute are not pure.

Fathers divide house and substance to their children, but a wife is wed to a man by God.

Cowardice possesses the hermaphrodite, and the mind of the lazy will starve.

He who keeps the commandment keeps his own mind, but he who despises his ways will perish.

He who pities the poor lends to God, and he will repay him according to his gift.

Chasten your son and he will be hopeful, and do not be exalted in your mind to haughtiness.

A malicious man will be severely punished, and if he commits injury, he will also lose his life.

Hear, son, the instruction of your father, that you may be wise at your latter end.

Many thoughts are in a man's heart, but the counsel of the Lord continues forever.

Mercy is a fruit to a man, and a poor man is better than a rich liar.

The fear of the Lord is life to a man, and he will lodge without fear in places where knowledge is not seen.

He who unjustly hides his hands in his chest, will not even bring them up to his mouth.

When a pestilent character is scourged, a simple man is made wiser, and if you reprove a wise man, he will understand discretion.

He who dishonors his father, and drives away his mother, will be disgraced and will be exposed to reproach.

A son who stops paying attention to the instructions of a father will love evil plans.

He who becomes responsible for a foolish child will despise the ordinance, and the mouth of ungodly men will drink down judgment.

Scourges are preparing for the intemperate, and punishments likewise for fools.

Proverbs: Chapter 20

Wine is an intemperate thing, and a strong drink full of violence, but every fool is entangled with them.

The threat of a king differs not from the rage of a lion, and he who provokes him sins against his own mind.

It is a glory to a man to turn aside from insulting, but every fool is entangled with such matters.

When a lazy one is reproached he is not ashamed, likewise, he who borrows grain in the harvest.

Counsel in a man's heart is deep water, but a prudent man will draw it out.

A man is valuable, and a merciful man is precious, but it is hard to find a faithful man.

He who walks blamelessly in justice will leave his children blessed.

Whenever a righteous king sits on the throne, no evil thing can stand before his presence.

Who will boast that he has a pure heart? Or who will boldly say that he is pure from sins?

A large or small weight with inconsistent measures are equally unclean before the Lord, and so is he who makes them.

A youth when in company with a godly man, will be restrained in his devices, and then his way will be straight.

The ear hears, and the eye sees, both of them are the Lord's work.

Love not speaking ill, or you may be cut off. Open your eyes, and be filled with bread.

The lamp of he that reviles father or mother will be put out, and his eyeballs will see darkness.

A portion hastily taken at first will not be blessed in the end.

Don't say, "I will avenge myself against my enemy," but wait for the Lord to help you.

A double weight is an abomination to the Lord, and a deceitful balance is not good in his sight.

A man's goings are directed by the Lord, so how then can a mortal understand his ways?

It is a snare to a man hastily to consecrate some of his own property, for in that case repentance comes after vowing.

A wise king completely crushes the ungodly and will bring a wheel on them.

The light of the Lord is in the person who searches his inmost parts.

Mercy and Truth are a guard to a king and will surround his throne with righteousness.

Wisdom is an ornament to young men, and gray hairs are the glory of old men.

Bruises and contusions befall bad men, and plagues will come in the inward parts of their bellies.

Proverbs: Chapter 21

Like a stream of water, so is the king's heart in God's hand, and he turns it wherever he may desire to point out.

Every man seems to himself righteous, but the Lord directs the hearts.

To be just and to speak the truth, are more pleasing to God than the blood of sacrifices.

A high-minded man is strong-hearted in his pride, and the lamp of the wicked is sin.

He who gathers treasures with a lying tongue pursues vanity into the snares of death.

The destruction will lodge with the ungodly, for they refuse to do justly.

To the disobedient, God sends disobedient ways, for his works are pure and right.

It is better to live on a corner of the house roof, than in plastered rooms with unrighteousness and in an open house.

The mind of the ungodly will not be pitied by any man.

When an intemperate man is punished the simple becomes wiser, and a man wise in understanding will receive knowledge.

A righteous man understands the hearts of the ungodly and despises the ungodly for their wickedness.

He who stops his ears from hearing the poor, himself also will cry, and there will be none to hear him.

A secret gift calms anger, but he who refuses to give stirs up strong anger.

It is the joy of the righteous to do justice, but a holy man is abominable with evil-doers.

A man that wanders out of the way of righteousness, will rest in the congregation of Rephaites.[1]

A poor man loves mirth, loving wine and oil in abundance, and a transgressor is the abomination of a righteous man.

It is better to live in a wilderness than with a quarrelsome talkative and passionate woman.

A desirable treasure will rest in the mouth of the wise, but foolish men will swallow it up.

The way of righteousness and mercy will find life and glory.

A wise man assaults strong cities and demolishes the fortress in which the ungodly trusted.

He who holds his mouth and his tongue keeps his mind from trouble.

A bold self-willed and insolent man is called a pest, and he who remembers injuries is a transgressor.

Desires kill the sluggard, for his hands do not choose to do anything.

An ungodly man entertains evil desires all day, but the righteous is unsparingly merciful and compassionate.

The sacrifices of the ungodly are an abomination to the Lord, for they offer them wickedly.

A false witness will perish, but an obedient man will speak cautiously.

An ungodly man impudently withstands with his face, but the upright man himself understands his ways.

There is no wisdom, there is no courage, there is no counsel against the ungodly.

A horse is prepared for the day of battle, but help is from the Lord.

Proverbs: Chapter 21 Notes

1 Codex Vaticanus: gigantôn (ΓΙΓΑΝΤΩΝ). Translation: Gigantes

• Aleppo Codex: rpåym (רפאים). Translation: sacred (plural form, or long dead)

- Leningrad Codex: refa'im (רְפָאִים). Translation: sacred (plural form, or long dead)

- Targum to Proverbs: benê arôā (בְּנֵי אַרְעָא). Translation: children of earth

In Greek mythology, the Gigantes were an ancient race of people who fought the gods and were destroyed. The term found in the Masoretic Text may have a similar origin, as the Raphaim were a quasi-mythical "long dead" people. The term was already in use in the Bronze Age Ugaritic Texts as well as later Iron Age Phoenician texts to refer to the "long dead." As the original text would not have mentioned the Greek Gigantes, the term Raphaim is imported from the Masoretic version, in the more common English translation of Rephaites.

Proverbs: Chapter 22

A fair name is better than much wealth, and good favor is above silver and gold.

The rich and the poor meet together, but the Lord made them both.

An intelligent man seeing a bad man severely punished is himself being instructed, but fools pass by and do not learn.

The fear of the Lord is the child of wisdom and wealth, and glory, and life.

Thistles and snares are in perverse ways, but he who keeps his mind will refrain from them.

The rich will rule over the poor, and servants will lend to their own masters.

He who sows wickedness will reap troubles, and will fully receive the punishment of his deeds.

God loves a cheerful and liberal man, but a man will prove the foolishness of his works.

He who has pity on the poor will himself be maintained, for he has given of his own bread to the poor.

He who gives liberally secures victory and honor, but he takes away the life of them that possess them.

Throw out a pestilent person from the council, and strife will go out with him, for when he sits in the council he dishonors all.

The Lord loves holy hearts, and all blameless persons are acceptable to him, a king rules with his lips.

The eyes of the Lord preserve discretion, but the transgressor despises wise words.

The sluggard makes excuses, and says, "There is a lion along the path and murderers in the streets."

The mouth of a transgressor is a deep pit, and he who is hated of the Lord will fall into it.

Evil ways are before a man, and he does not like to turn away from them, but it is needful to turn aside from a perverse and bad way.

Foolishness is attached to the heart of a child, but the wand and instruction are then far from him.

He who oppresses the poor increases his own substance yet gives to the rich to make it less.

Incline your ear to the words of wise men, hear also my word, and apply your heart, that you may know that they are good, and if you lay them to heart, they will also gladden you on your lips.

That your trust may be in the Lord, and he may make your way known to you.

You too repeatedly record them for yourself on the table of your heart, for counsel and knowledge.[1]

I, therefore, teach you truth, and knowledge which is good to hear, that you may answer words of truth to them that question you.

Do no violence to the poor, for he is needy, nor dishonor the helpless man at the gates.

The Lord will plead his cause, and you will deliver your mind in safety.

Do not be a companion to a furious man, nor lodge with a passionate man, in case you learn of his ways, and get snares to your mind.

Don't become responsible in respect of a man's debts, because if they don't know where to get compensation from, they will take the bed that is under you.

Don't remove the old landmarks which your forefathers erected.

It is fit that an observant man and one diligent in his business should attend on kings, and not attend on slothful men.

Proverbs: Chapter 22 Notes

1 This verse is entirely different from the verse in the Masoretic version: halo chatavti lecha [shilshovm] (shalishim) bemov'etzot vada'at (הֲלֹא כָתַבְתִּי לְךָ [שִׁלְשׁוֹם] (שָׁלִישִׁים) בְּמֹעֵצֹת (שְׁלִישִׁים) [שִׁלְשׁוֹם] וָדָעַת) which was translated as "Have not I written to thee excellent things in counsels and knowledge," in the King James Version. Once the Wisdom of Amenemope was translated, it became apparent that sections of Proverbs chapter 22 and 23 were significantly similar to Amenemope, and likely taken from a Phoenician translation of Amenemope.

It is now accepted that there is a copyist's error in the Hebrew text, which was corrected via comparison to Amenemope to "Have I not written for you thirty sayings of counsel and knowledge" in the English Standard Version of the Bible. As the Greek translation has a significantly different verse from the Hebrew, it is clear that the translators at Alexandria did not understand the Aramaic text either, which implies that the error was already present by that time, probably dating back to the Phoenician translation.

Proverbs: Chapter 23

If you sit to eat at the table of a prince, consider atten- tively the things set before you and apply your hand, knowing that it behooves you to prepare such food, but even if you are very insatiable, don't desire his provi- sions, for these belong to a false life.

If you are poor, don't compare yourself to a rich man, but refrain yourself in your wisdom. If you should fix your eye on him, he will disappear, for wings like an eagle's are prepared for him, and he returns to the house of his master.

Do not eat with an envious man, and don't desire his food. He eats and drinks like anyone who could swallow a hair. Don't invite him to yourself, or eat your food with him, for he will vomit it up, and spoil your fair words.

Say nothing in the ears of a fool, in case at any time he sneers at your wise words.

Do not remove the ancient landmarks, and don't enter on the possession of the fatherless, for the Lord is their protector, he is mighty and will plead their cause with you.

Apply your heart to instruction, and prepare your ears for words of discretion.

Do not refrain from educating a child, for if you beat him with the stick, he will not die. For you will beat him with the stick and will deliver his mind from death.

Son, if your heart is wise, you will also gladden my heart, and your lips will converse with my lips if they are right.

Don't let your heart envy sinners, but be afraid of the Lord all day.

For if you should keep these things, you have posterity, and your hope will not be removed.

Hear, my son, and be wise, and rightly direct the thoughts of your heart.

Do not be a drunkard, neither staying late at feasts, nor purchases of flesh, for every drunkard and whore-monger, will be poor, and every sluggard will clothe himself with tatters and ragged garments.

Listen, my son, to your father who fathered you, and don't hate your mother because she is grown old. A righteous father brings up his children well, and his mind rejoices over a wise son.

Let your father and your mother rejoice over you, and let her who carried you be happy.

Son, give me your heart and let your eyes observe my ways.

For a strange house is a vessel full of holes, and a strange well is narrow.

One like this will perish suddenly, and every transgressor will be cut off.

Who has woe? Who trouble? Who has quarrels? Who vexations and disputes? Who has bruises without a cause? Whose eyes are livid? Are not those of them that stay long at wine? Are not those of them that haunt the places where banquets are?

Do not be drunk with wine, but converse with just men, and converse with them openly. For if you should set your eyes on bowls and cups, you will afterwards go more naked than a pestle.

In the end, one like this lays down just like one bit by a serpent, with venom diffused through him (as if by a horned serpent.)

Whenever your eyes will see a strange woman, then your mouth will speak perverse things.

You will lie as among the sea and as a pilot in a great storm.

You will say, "They struck me, and I was not pained, and they mocked me, and I did not know it." When it is morning, you may go and seek them, and see with whom they keep company.

Proverbs: Chapter 24

Son, don't envy bad men or desire to be with them. For their heart conceives lies, and their lips speak injuries.

A house is built by wisdom and is set up by understanding. By discretion, the chambers are filled with all precious and excellent wealth.

A wise man is better than a strong man, and a man who has prudence than a large estate.

War is planned by generals, and aid is supplied to the heart of a counselor.

Wisdom and good understanding are in the gates of the wise, the wise don't turn away from the mouth of the Lord, but deliberate in council.

Death befalls uninstructed men. The fools also die in sins, and uncleanness attaches to a pestilent man. He will be defiled on the evil day, and on the day of affliction until he is completely consumed.

Deliver those who are led away to death, and redeem those who are appointed to be slain, don't spare your help. But if you should say, "I don't know this man," know that the Lord knows the hearts of all, and he who formed breath for all. He knows all things, who renders to every man according to his works.

Son, eat honey, for the honeycomb is good, so your throat may be sweetened, and will you perceive wisdom in your mind. If you find it, your end will be good, and hopefully will not fail you.

Don't bring an ungodly man in among the righteous, nor be deceived by the feeding of the belly. A righteous man will fall seven times and rise again, but the ungodly will be without strength in troubles.

If your enemy should fall, don't rejoice over him or be elated at his downfall. The Lord will see it, and it will not please him, and he will turn his anger away from him.

Do not celebrate evil-doers, nor be envious of sinners. For the evil man has no posterity, and the light of the wicked will be put out.

Son, fear God and the king, and do not disobey either of them, for they will suddenly punish the ungodly, and who can know the vengeance inflicted by both?

A son that keeps the commandment will escape destruction, for one like this has fully received it.

Let no falsehood be spoken by the king from the tongue, yes, let no falsehood proceed from his tongue.

The king's tongue is a sword, and not one of flesh, and whoever will be given up to it will be destroyed, for if his anger should be provoked, he destroys men with cords and devours men's bones, and burns them up like a flame so that they are not even fit to be eaten by the young eagles.

Son, revere my words, receive them and repent.

This thing I say to you, would be wise for you to learn. It is not good to have the respect of persons in judgment.

He who says of the ungodly, 'He is righteous,' will be cursed by peoples, and hateful among the nations. But they who disapprove of him will appear more excellent, and blessing will come on them, and men will kiss lips that answer well.

Prepare your works for your going out, and prepare yourself for the field, and come after me, and you will rebuild your house.

Do not be a false witness against your fellow citizen, nor exaggerate with your lips.

Do not say, "As he has treated me, so will I treat him, and I will avenge myself on him for that in which he has injured me."

A foolish man is like a farm, and a senseless man is like a vineyard. If you leave him alone, he will altogether remain barren and covered with weeds, and he becomes destitute, and his stone walls are broken down.

Afterwards, I reflected, I looked that I might receive instruction.

The sluggard says, "I slumber a little, and I sleep a little, and for a little while I fold my arms across my chest."

But if you do this, your poverty will come speedily, and your lack like a swift courier.

Proverbs: Chapter 25

These are the genuine instructions of Solomon, which the friends of King Hezekiah of Judah copied out.

The glory of God conceals a matter, but the glory of a king honors business.

The sky is high, and Earth is deep, and a king's heart is unsearchable.

Beat the worthless silver, and it will be made entirely pure.

Slay the ungodly from before the king, and his throne will prosper in righteousness.

Do not be boastful in the presence of the king, and don't remain in the places of princes, as it is better for you that it should be said, 'Come up to me,' than that one should humiliate you in the presence of the prince.

Speak of that which your eyes have seen.

Do not get suddenly into a quarrel, in case you regret it later.

Whenever your friend insults you, step back and don't despise him. If your friend continues to insult you and your quarrel and disagreement will not end, it will be like death for you.

Choose friendship and set a man free, who you keep for yourself, or you may become liable to reproach. Pay attention to keep your ways peaceably.

Like a golden apple in a necklace of sardius, likewise is it to speak a wise word.

In an ear-ring of gold a precious sardius is also set, and likewise a wise word is to an obedient ear.

As a fall of snow in the time of harvest is good against heat, so a faithful messenger refreshes those that send him, for he helps the minds of his employers.

As winds and clouds and rains are the most evident objects, so is he who boasts of a false gift.

With patience, comes prosperity to kings, and a soft tongue breaks the bones.

Having found honey, eat only what is enough, in case unwisely you are filled, and vomit it up.

Enter sparingly into your friend's house, in case he is satiated with your company, and hates you.

As a club, and a dagger, and a pointed arrow, so also is a man who bears false witness against his friend.

The way of the wicked and the foot of the transgressor will perish on a terrible day.

As vinegar is bad for a sore, trouble befalling the body afflicts the heart.

Like a moth in a garment and a worm in wood, so the grief of a man hurts the heart.

If your enemy hungers, feed him, if he thirsts, give him drink, for so doing you will heap coals of fire on his head, and the Lord will reward you with good.

The north wind raises clouds, so an impudent face provokes the tongue.

It is better to live on a corner of the roof, than with an insulting woman in an open house.

Like cold water is agreeable to a thirsting mind, so is a good message from a land far off.

As if one should stop a well, and corrupt a spring of water, so is it unseemly for a righteous man to fall before an ungodly man.

It is not good to eat much honey, but it is right to honor venerable sayings.

Like a city whose walls are broken down, and which is unfortified, so is a man who does anything without counsel.

Proverbs: Chapter 26

Like dew in harvest, and as rain in summer, so honor is not seemly for a fool.

Like birds and sparrows fly, likewise a curse will not come on anyone without a cause.

Like a whip for a horse, and a goad for a donkey, so is a wand for a simple nation.

Don't reply to a fool according to his foolishness, in case you become like him.

Yet answer a fool according to his foolishness, in case he seems wise in his own conceit.

He who sends a message by a foolish messenger procures for himself a reproach from his ways.

As well, take away the motion of the legs, as transgression from the mouth of fools.

He who binds up a stone in a sling is like one who gives glory to a fool.

Thorns grow in the hand of a drunkard, and servitude in the hand of fools.

All the flesh of fools endures much hardship, for their fury is brought to nothing.

Like when a dog goes to his own vomit and becomes abominable, so is a fool who returns in his wickedness to his own sin.

There is a shame that brings sin, and there is a shame that is glory and grace.

I have seen a man who seemed to himself to be wise, but a fool had more hope than he.

A sluggard when sent on a journey says, "There is a lion along the road, and there are murderers in the streets."

As a door turns on the hinge, so does a sluggard on his bed.

A sluggard having hidden his hand in his chest, will not be able to bring it up to his mouth.

A sluggard seems to himself wiser than one who most satisfactorily brings back a message.

Like he who lays hold of a dog's tail, so is he who makes himself the champion of another's cause.

Like those who need correction put out nice words to men, and he who first falls in with the proposal will be overthrown, so are all that lay wait for their own friends, and when they are discovered, say, "I was just joking."

With much wood fire increases, but where there is not a two-faced man, strife ceases.

A hearth for coals, and wood for the fire, and insulting man for the tumult of strife.

The words of cunning knaves are soft, but they strike even to the inmost parts of the bowels.

Silver dishonestly given is to be considered as a potsherd, smooth lips cover a terrible heart.

A weeping enemy promises all things with his lips, but in his heart, he contrives deceit.

Though your enemy entreats you with a loud voice, don't consent, for there are seven abominations in his heart.

He who hides enmity frames deceit, but being easily discerned exposes his own sins in the public assemblies.

He who digs a pit for his neighbor will fall into it, and he who rolls a stone, rolls it on himself.

A lying tongue hates the truth, and an unguarded mouth causes trouble.

Proverbs: Chapter 27

Do not brag about tomorrow, for you don't know what the next day will bring.

Let your neighbor, and not your own mouth, praise you, a stranger, and not your own lips.

A stone is heavy and sand cumbersome, but a fool's anger is heavier than both.

Anger is merciless, and anger sharp, but envy can carry nothing.

Open disapproval is better than secret love.

The wounds of a friend are more to be trusted than the spontaneous kisses of an enemy.

A full mind scorns honeycombs, but to a hungry mind, even bitter things appear sweet.

As when a bird flies down from its own nest, so a man is brought into slavery whenever he estranges himself from his own place.

The heart delights in ointments and wines and perfumes, but the mind is broken by calamities.

Don't ignore your own friend or your father's friend, and when you are in distress don't go into your brother's house. A close friend is better than a distant brother.

Son, be wise, so your heart may rejoice, and remove yourself from reproachful words.

A wise man, when evils are approaching, hides, but fools pass on and will be punished.

Take away the man's garment, (for a scorner has passed by) whoever lays waste to another's goods.

Whoever will bless a friend in the morning with a loud voice, will seem to differ nothing from one who curses him.

On a stormy day drops of rain drive a man out of his house, so also does an insulting woman drive a man out of his own house.

The north wind is sharp, but it is called propitious.

Iron sharpens iron, and a man sharpens his friend's attitude.

He who plants a fig tree will eat the fruits of it, so he who waits on his own master will be honored.

As faces are not like other faces, neither are the thoughts of men.

Sheol and destruction are not filled, and so also are the eyes of men insatiable.

He who fixes his eye is an abomination to the Lord, and the uninstructed do not restrain their tongue.

Fire is the trial for silver and gold, and a man is tried by the mouth of them that praise him.

The heart of the transgressor seeks after injuries, but an upright heart seeks knowledge.

Though you scourge a fool, disgracing him among the council, you will still in no way remove his foolishness from him.

Do you thoroughly know the number of your flock, and pay attention to your herds?

A man does not have strength and power forever, neither does he transmit it from generation to generation.

Take care of the plants in the field and you will cut grass. Gather the mountain hay, so you may have sheep's wool for clothing. Pay attention to the land, so you may have lambs.

Son, you have very useful words from me, for both your life and the life of your servants.

Proverbs: Chapter 28

The ungodly man flees when no one pursues, but the righteous is as confident as a lion.

Because of the sins of ungodly men quarrels rise, but a wise man will quell them.

A bold man oppresses the poor by ungodly deeds.

As an impetuous and profitable rain, so they who forsake the law praise ungodliness, but they who love the law fortify themselves with a wall.

Evil men will not understand judgment, but they who seek the Lord will understand everything.

A poor man walking in truth is better than a rich liar.

A wise son keeps the law, but he who keeps up debauchery dishonors his father.

He who increases his wealth through interest and unjust gains gathers it for him who pities the poor.

He who turns away his ear from hearing the law, even he has made his prayer abominable.

He who causes upright men to err in an evil way, himself will fall into destruction. The transgressor also will pass by prosperity, but will not enter into it.

A rich man is wise in his own conceit, but an intelligent poor man will condemn him.

Because of the help of righteous men great glory arises, but in the places of the ungodly men are caught.

He who covers his own ungodliness will not prosper, but he who blames himself will be loved.

Blessed is the man who religiously fears always, but the hard of heart will fall into injuries.

A hungry lion and a thirsty wolf is he, who, being poor, rules over a poor nation.

A king in need of revenues is a great oppressor, but he who hates injustice will live a long time.

He who becomes responsible for a man ordered with murder will be an exile, and not in safety.

Chasten your son, and he will love you and give honor to your mind, he will not obey a sinful nation.

He who walks justly is assisted, but he who walks in crooked ways will be entangled in them.

He who tills his own land will be satisfied with bread, but he who follows idleness has plenty of poverty.

A man worthy of credit will be blessed greatly, but the wicked will not go unpunished.

He who does not revere the just is not good. One like this will sell a man for a morsel of bread.

An envious man rushes to become rich and doesn't know that the merciful man has mastery over him.

He who disapproves of a man's ways has more favor than he who flatters with the tongue.

He who abandons his father or mother, and thinks he does not sin will partake with an ungodly man.

An unbelieving man judges rashly, but he who trusts in the Lord will act carefully.

He who trusts in a bold heart is a fool, but he who walks in wisdom will be safe.

He who gives to the poor will not be in poverty, but he who turns away his eye from him will be in great distress.

In the places of ungodly men the righteous mourn, but in their destruction, the righteous will be multiplied.

Proverbs: Chapter 29

A disapprover is better than a stubborn man, for when the latter is suddenly set on fire, there will be no remedy.

When the righteous are praised, the people will rejoice, but when the ungodly rule, men mourn.

When a man loves wisdom, his father rejoices, but he who keeps prostitutes will waste wealth.

A righteous king establishes a country, but a transgressor destroys it.

He who prepares a net in the way of his friend entangles his own feet in it.

A great snare is spread for a sinner, but the righteous will be in joy and gladness.

A righteous man knows how to judge in favor of the poor, but the ungodly understands not knowledge, and the poor man has not an understanding mind.

Lawless men burn down a city, but wise men turn away anger.

A wise man will judge nations, but a worthless man being angry laughs and fears not.

Bloody men hate a holy person, but the upright will seek his mind.

A fool speaks everything on his mind, but the wise hold something back.

When a king listens to unjust language, all his subjects are transgressors.

When the creditor and debtor meet together, the Lord oversees them both.

When a king judges the poor in truth, his throne will be established for a testimony.

Stripes and disapproval give wisdom, but an erring child disgraces his parents.

When the ungodly abound, sins abound, but when they fall, the righteous are warned.

Chasten your son, and he will give you rest, and he will give honor to your mind.

There will be no interpreter to a sinful nation, but he who observes the law is blessed.

A stubborn servant will not be reproved by words, for even if he understands, still he will not obey.

If you see a man hasty in his words, know that the fool has hope rather than he.

He who lives wantonly from a child will be a servant, and in the end, will grieve over himself.

A furious man stirs up strife, and a passionate man digs up sin.

Pride brings a man low, but the Lord upholds the humiliate-minded with honor.

He who shares with a thief hates his own mind, and if any had heard an oath uttered tell not of it, they fearing and reverencing men unreasonably have been over-thrown, but he who trusts in the Lord will rejoice.

Ungodliness causes a man to stumble, but he who trusts in his master will be safe.

Many wait on the favor of rulers, but justice comes to a man from the Lord.

A righteous man is an abomination to an unrighteous man, and the direct way is an abomination to the sinner.

Proverbs: Chapter 30

These sayings are for the man to hear them who trusts in God, and I stop here. I am the simplest of all men, and there is not in me the wisdom of men. God has taught me wisdom, and I know the knowledge of the sacred. Who has gone up to the sky, and come down? Who has gathered the winds in his chest? Who has wrapped up the waters in a garment? Who has dominion over all the ends of the Earth? What is his name? What are the name of his children? For all the words of God are tested in the fire, and he defends those who revere him. Don't add to his words, in case he tests you, and you are proved a liar. Two things I ask of you and take no favor from me before I die. Leave far from me vanity and falsehood, and give me neither wealth nor poverty, but appoint me what is needful and sufficient in case I become filled and become false, and say, "Who sees me?" or become poor and steal, and swear vainly by the name of God.

Don't deliver a servant into the hands of his master, in case he curses you, and you are completely destroyed. A wicked generation curses their father and does not bless their mother. A wicked generation judges themselves to be just, but do not cleanse their way. A wicked generation has lofty eyes and exalts themselves with their eyelids. A wicked generation has swords for teeth and jaws for knives, to destroy and devour the lowly from the earth, and the poor from among men. The leech had three dearly beloved daughters, and these three did not satisfy her, and the fourth was not contented to say, "Sheol and the woman he loves, and Tiamat and Eretz are not surrounded by water," and "water and fire would never say 'enough.'"

The eye that laughs to mock a father, and dishonors the old age of a mother, let the ravens of the valleys pick it out and let the young eagles devour it. Moreover, there are three things impossible for me to comprehend, and the fourth I don't know, the track of a flying eagle, the ways of a serpent on a rock, and the paths of a ship passing through the sea, and the ways of a man in youth. Such is the way of an adulterous woman, who having washed from what she has done, says she has done nothing incorrectly.

By three things the earth is troubled, and the fourth it can't carry: if a servant reigns or a fool is filled with food, or if a maidservant should throw out her own mistress, or if a hateful woman should marry a good man.

There are four very little things on the earth, but these are wiser than the wise: the ants which are weak and yet prepare their food in summer, the rabbits also are a feeble race who make their houses in the rocks, the locusts have no king, and yet march orderly at one command, and the newt, which supports itself by its hands and is easily captured, yet dwells in the fortresses of kings.

There are three things that go well, and a fourth which passes along finely: a lion's cub is stronger than all other beasts and does not turn away nor fear any beast, a cock walking in boldly among the hens, the goat leading the herd, and a king publicly speaking before a nation.

If you abandon yourself to joking and reach out your hand in a fight, you will be disgraced.

Milk out milk, and there will be butter, and if you hit one's nostrils there will come out blood, so if you extort words, there will come forth quarrels and strife.

Proverbs: Chapter 30 Notes

1 Codex Vaticanus: Adês cae erôs gynaecos cae Tartaros cae Gê ouc empiplamenê ydatos cae ydôr cae pyr ou mê ipôsin arci (ΑΔΗC ΚΑΙ ΕΡѠC ΓΥΝΑΙΚΟC ΚΑΙ ΤΑΡΤΑΡΟC ΚΑΙ ΓΗ ΟΥΚ ΕΜΠΙΠΤΛΑΜΕΝΗ ΥΔΑΤΟC ΚΑΙ ΥΔѠΡ ΚΑΙ ΠΥΡ ΟΥ ΜΗ ΕΙΠѠCΙΝ ΑΡΚΕΙ). Translation: Hades and the woman he loves and Tartatus and Ge are not surrounded by water and water and fire would never say enough.

• Aleppo Codex: šåůl ůôṣr-rḥm årṣ lå-šbôh mym ůåš lå-åmrh hůn (שאול ועצר-רחם ארץ לא-שבעה מים ואש לא-אמרה הון).

Translation: Sheol (or Saul) and trapple the compasionate Eretz not seven waters and fire never said enough

- Leningrad Codex: she'ol ve'otzer racham eretz lo-save'ah mayim lo-amerah hon (שְׁאוֹל וְעֹצֶר רֶחַם אֶרֶץ לֹא־שָׂבְעָה מַּיִם לֹא־אָמְרָה הוֹן). Translation: Sheol (or Saul) and stop (or arrrest) the womb of Eretz (or land) not seven waters and fire never said enough

- Targum to Proverbs: šeyôl weahădat rahămê wearā lā śābeā mayā wenûrā lā āmerâ mistā (שִׁיוֹל וְאַחֲדַת רַחֲמֵי וְאַרְעָא לָא שָׂבְעָא מַיָא וְנוּרָא לָא אָמְרָה מִסְתָּא). Translation: grave (or netherworld) and three compasionate (or merciful) and land not ask (or pray) water and tremble (or fear) and not said enough

The Greek, Hebrew, and Judeo-Aramaic translations are not consistent, and the meaning of the verse was probably forgotten before the translations were made. The Greeks seemed to interpret it as a reference to Hades and Persephone, Tartatus, and Ge not being surrounded by water. It is unclear if there was something along the lines of Persephone in the Aramaic text they worked from or if they misunderstood the text. The closest Canaanite equivalent of Persephone was the goddess Adamah (אדמה), who was in the Masoretic version of the book of Numbers. Both Eretz and Adamah were translated as "Ge" (Γη) meaning "Earth" or "Gaia" in the Septuagint's version of Numbers, suggesting she was in the verse, and the Greeks didn't know how to translate the name. While Hades and Ge are mirrored by Sheol and Eretz in the Hebrew translation, and Tartatus by

Tiamat, earlier in Proverbs, Adamah is conjectural, and so her name is not used in this translation.

Proverbs: Chapter 31

My words have been spoken by God, the oracular answer of a king, whose mother instructed. What will you keep, my son, what? The words of God. My first-born son, I speak to you: what? Son of my womb? What? Son? Of my vows? Do not give your wealth to women, nor your mind, and live to regret. Do all things with counsel, drink wine with counsel. Princes are prone to anger, don't let them drink wine in case they drink, and forget wisdom and are not able to judge the poor rightly. Give a strong drink to those that are in sorrow, and the wine as a drink to those in pain, that they may forget their poverty, and may not remember their troubles anymore.

Open your mouth with the word of God, and judge all fairly. Open your mouth and judge justly, and plead the cause of the poor and weak. Who will find a virtuous woman? Such a one is more valuable than precious gems. The heart of her husband trusts in her, such a one will stand in no need of fine spoils. For she employs all her living for her husband's good. Gathering wool and flax, she makes it serviceable with her hands. She is like a ship trading from a distance, so she procures her livelihood. She rises by night and gives food to her household, and appointed tasks to her maidens. She views a farm and buys it, and with the fruit of her hands, she plants a possession. She strongly girds her loins and strengthens her arms for work. She finds by experience that working is good, and her candle does not go out all night. She reaches out her arms to needful works and applies her hands to the spindle. She opens her hands to the needy and hands out fruit to the poor.

Her husband is not anxious about those at home when he delays anywhere abroad, for all her household are clothed. She makes for her husband clothes of double texture, and garments for herself of fine linen and scarlet. Her husband becomes a distinguished person at the gates when he sits on the council with the old inhabitants of the land. She makes fine linens and sells girdles to the Canaanites. She opens her mouth heedfully and with propriety, and controls her tongue. She puts on strength and honor and rejoices in the last days. But she opens her mouth wisely, and according to the law. The ways of her household are careful, and she does not eat the bread of idleness. Her kindness to them sets up her children for them, and they grow rich, and her husband praises her.

Many daughters have obtained wealth, and many have worked valiantly, but you have exceeded, you have surpassed all. Charms are false, and woman's beauty is vain, for it is a wise woman that is blessed, and let her praise the fear the Lord. Give her the fruit of her lips, and let her husband be praised in the gates.

Ecclesiastes: Chapter 1

The words of the High Queen,[1] of the son of David, king of Israel in Jerusalem.

"Vanity of vanities," said the apostle, "Vanity of vanities, All is vanity. What advantage is there to a man in all the labor that he takes under the sun? A generation goes, and a generation comes, but the Earth stands forever. The Sun arises, and the Sun goes down and draws towards its place, arising there it proceeds southward and goes up towards the north. The wind goes round and round, and the wind returns to its paths. All the rivers run into the sea, and yet the sea is not filled to the place from where the rivers come, and to which they return again. All things are full of labor. A man will not be able to describe them. Neither will the eye be satisfied by seeing them nor will the ear be filled by hearing them. What is that which has been? The same thing which will be, and what is that which has always been. The very thing which will always be, and there is nothing new under the sun."

"Who is it that will say, 'Look, this is new?' It has already been in the ages that have passed before us. There is no memory of the first things. Neither will the things that are most recent be remembered by those who will exist at the end of time. I the apostle, was a king over Israel in Jerusalem. I applied my heart to seek out and examine by wisdom concerning all things that are done under the sky, for God[2] has given to the sons of men evil trouble to be bothered by. I saw all the works that were worked under the Sun, and, saw, all were vanity and waywardness of spirit. That which is crooked can't be made straight, and deficit can't be counted. I spoke in my heart, saying, 'Look, I am increased, and have acquired wisdom beyond all who were before me in Jerusalem,' also I applied my heart to know wisdom and knowledge. My heart knew much wisdom, knowledge, parables, and understanding. I perceived that this also is the waywardness of spirit. For in the abundance of wisdom is an abundance of knowledge, and he that increases knowledge will increase sorrow."

Ecclesiastes: Chapter 1 Notes

1 Codex Vaticanus: ecclêsiastou (ЄΚΚΛΗΟΙΑϹΤΟΥ)

• Aleppo Codex: qhlt (קֹהֶלֶת)

• Leningrad Codex: kohelet (קֹהֶלֶת)

• Targum to Ecclesiastes: deitnabbā qōhelet (דְּאִתְנַבָּא קֹהֶלֶת). Translation: prophecy of Qohelet

The word ecclêsiastou (ЄΚΚΛΗΟΙΑϹΤΟΥ) does not have a direct translation into English, but would be approximately "female cleric."

The Masoretic term Kohelet (קֹהֶלֶת) is treated as a name or pseudonym of the author of the text. Christian translators have generally translated the term as "preacher" or "teacher," although the exact meaning is unclear. It is a feminine term, however, there is no clear Canaanite or Aramaic root word that seems applicable. The Classical era Hebrew term qhl (קהל) means "community," or "audience." The Aramaic Targum treats Qohelet as the name of a prophet.

The Masoretic term probably originated in the Egyptian term qảỉ ḥnůt (𓂧𓄿𓇋 𓎼𓏏), meaning "high queen," suggesting the author was Solomon's first wife. If qảỉ ḥnůt were transliterated directly into Canaanite in the era of Solomon, it would have been qhnt (𐤕𐤍𐤇𐤒), which could have been rendered as qhlt (קהלת) by mistransliterating an L (ל) for an N (𐤍).

2 Codex Vaticanus: o theos (ΟΘΕΟС). Translation: the god

• Aleppo Codex: ålhym (אלהים). Translation: gods (in Aramaic, goddesses in Hebrew, god in Assyrian)

• Leningrad Codex: elohim (אֱלֹהִים). Translations: gods (in Aramaic, goddesses in Hebrew, god in Assyrian)

• Targum to Ecclesiastes: yeyā (??). Translation: Yhů

The Masoretic word is commonly translated as "God," but is a plural form of the Aramaic ålhå (𐡀𐡄𐡋𐡀), meaning "gods," or a plural form of the Hebrew elah (אֱלָה) meaning "goddesses."

The terms ålhym (𐤌𐤉𐤄𐤋𐤀) and ålhym (𐡌𐡉𐡄𐡋𐡀) are also direct transcriptions of the Neo-Assyrian word elium

(𒀭𒉌𒈹), which by the Iron Age meant "god," indicating that text had previously been written in cuneiform, and was translated into Aramaic or Phoenician during the iron age. During the bronze age, the word alium (𒀭𒈨𒋛𒈠), and referred to a specific god, ^{deity}Ān (✴✴) the highest god, and father of the other gods. His Akkadian name was derived from the word elûm (𒀭𒈨𒈨), meaning 'higher,' as the term was intended to convey the meaning of 'highest.' He was believed to live in the polar region of the sky, where the modern constellation of Draco is located, making him the highest in the sky, around which all the gods (stars) circled.

The term el elyovn (אֵל עֶלְיוֹן), meaning "highest god," was translated into Hebrew in Bereshít Chapter 14, where the Greeks translated it as Theô tô hypsistô (Θεῷ τῷ ὑψίστῳ) in Cosmic Genesis, also meaning "highest god." El Elyon is known to have been a major god of the Canaanites, called ȧl ůȧlyn (𐤉𐤋𐤏 𐤋𐤀), meaning "God and Highest" in an Aramaic language Sefire Treaty from circa 750 BC. The Greek translations of Sanchuniathon's Bronze Age writing that have survived to the present, referred to the primordial creator god of the Canaanites as Elioun (Ελιουν), which appears to be the same god. According to Sanchuniathon, Elioun was the highest (ύψιστος) god, who made the sky and the land, and they made the rest of the gods.

During the Old Babylonian and Old Assyrian eras, the gods Marduk and Ashur, the national gods of Babylon and Assyria, replaced the Akkadian An as the primary god of the Mesopotamian pantheons, and by the Iron Age, the word elium had come to mean "god," explaining why the Aramaic term ålhym (𐤉𐤄𐤋𐤀) would have been interpreted as "god," by the Greeks. This means that the origin of Cosmic Genesis chapter 1 would have to have been in the Sumerian or Akkadian era, before the emergence of the Old Babylonian empire, and that the form of Cuneiform it was written in before being translated into Aramaic and Canaanite was Old Akkadian.

Ecclesiastes: Chapter 2

"I said in my heart, 'Come now, and I will relieve you with humor,' and pay attention, and, look, this too was vanity. I said to laughter, 'Madness!' and to humor, 'Why do you do this?' I examined whether my heart would excite my flesh like wine, (though my heart guided me in wisdom,) and I desired to lay hold of joy until I should see what good it is for the sons of men that they should work under the sun all the days of their life. I enlarged my work. I built houses. I planted vineyards. I made gardens and orchards and planted in them every kind of fruit tree. I made pools of water to water them from out of the timber-bearing wood. I got slaves and women slaves, and slaves were born to me in my house. Also, I had many flocks and herds, greater than all who came before me in Jerusalem. Moreover, I collected for myself both silver and gold and also the peculiar treasures of kings and provinces. I procured singing men and singing women, and delights of the sons of men: a butler and female cup-bearers."

"I became great and wealthier than all who came before me in Jerusalem, and also my wisdom was granted to me. Whatever my eyes desired, I did not hold back from them. I did not hold back my heart from all my joy, for my heart rejoiced in all my work, and this was my portion of all my labor. I looked on all my works which my hands had worked, and on my work which I labored to perform, and look, all was vanity and grasping for wind, and there is no advantage under the sun."

"Then I searched to find wisdom, madness, and foolishness, for who is the man who will search after counsel, in all things in which he employs it? I saw that wisdom is greater than foolishness, as much as light is greater than darkness. The wise man's eyes are in his head, but the fool walks in darkness. I perceived, even I, that one event would happen to them both. I said in my heart, 'As the event of the fool, so will it be for me, even me! Why have I gained wisdom?' I also said in my heart, 'This is also vanity because the fool speaks of his abundance. There is no memory of the wise man or the fool forever, and in the coming days, all things will be forgotten. How will the wise man die, or the fool?"

"I hated life because the work that was worked under the sun[1] was evil to me. All is vanity and grasping for the wind. I hated all of the work that I did under the Sun because I had to leave it to the man who would come after me. Who knows whether he will be a wise man or a fool? Or whether he has power over all my work in which I labored, and in which I grew wise under the sun?"

"This is also vanity. So I went out to dismiss from my heart all my works which I had labored under the sun.

For there is such a man that his labor is wisdom, knowledge, and fortitude, yet this man will give his portion to
one who has not labored in those fields. This is also
vanity and a great evil. For it happens to a man in all his
labor, and in the purpose of his heart in which he labors
under the sun. For all his days are days of sorrows, and
trouble of spirit is his. In the night also his heart does not
rest."

"This is also vanity. A man has nothing really good to
eat or to drink, and to show his mind[2] something good
during his trouble. This also I saw, that it is from the
hand of God. For who will eat, or who will drink,
without him? For God has given to the man who is good
in his sight, wisdom, and knowledge, and joy, but he has
given to the sinner trouble, to add and to heap up, that
he may give to him that is good before God, for this is
also vanity and waywardness of spirit."

Ecclesiastes: Chapter 2 Notes

1 Codex Vaticanus: êlion (ΗΛΙΟΝ). Translation: sun (or
Helios)

- Dead Sea Scroll 4QQoh[b]: ăšr (אשר)

- Aleppo Codex: šmš (שמש). Translation: sun (or Shemesh)

- Leningrad Codex: shamesh (שֶׁמֶשׁ). Translation: sun (or
Shemesh)

- Targum to Ecclesiastes: šimšā (שִׁמְשָׁא). Translation: sun (or servant)

The deviation in 4QQoh[b] is not an obvious Semitic substitution for "sun," but could date to a Neo-Assyrian translation, as Aššur (𒀸𒋩) was the name of the supreme Assyrian god, who was also depicted as the winged sun.

2 Codex Vaticanus: psychê (ΨΥΧΗ). Translation: mind (or personality, psyche)

- Aleppo Codex: npš (נפש). Translation: mind (or life, psyche, person)

- Leningrad Codex: nafsh (נָפְשׁ). Translation: mind (or life, psyche, person)

- Targum to Ecclesiastes: napšē (נַפְשֵׁ). Translation: mind (or life, psyche, person)

Ecclesiastes: Chapter 3

"To all things, there is a time and a season for every matter under the sky."[1]

"A time of birth, and a time to die."

"A time to plant, and a time to reap what has been sown."

"A time to kill, and a time to heal."

"A time to tear down, and a time to build up."

"A time to cry, and a time to laugh."

"A time to lament, and a time to dance."

"A time to throw stones, and a time to gather stones together."

"A time to embrace, and a time to abstain from embracing."

"A time to seek, and a time to lose."

"A time to keep, and a time to throw away."

"A time to rip, and a time to sew."

"A time to be silent, and a time to speak."

"A time to love, and a time to hate."

"A time of war, and a time of peace."

"What advantage has he that works, from those things in which he labors? I have seen all the trouble that God has given to the sons of men to be bothered with. All the things that he has made are beautiful in his time. He has also set the whole world in their heart, so that man might not find out the work which God has worked from the beginning even to the end. I know that there is no good in them, except for a man to rejoice, and to do good in his life. Also in the case of every man who will eat and drink, and see good in all his labor, this is a gift of God. I know that whatever things God has done, they will be forever. It is impossible to add to it, and it is impossible to take away from it. God has done it, so men may be in fear before him. That which has been is now, and whatever things have been appointed to be, have already been, and God will remember that which is past."

"Moreover, I saw under the Sun the place of judgment. There was the ungodly one, and the place of righteousness, and there was the godly one. I said in my heart, 'God will judge the righteous and the ungodly, for there is a time there for every action and every work.' I said in my heart, 'Concerning the speech of the sons of man, God will judge them, and also to those that are beasts. Both the sons of man, and the animals, one event befalls them both, as the death of the one is, so also is the death of the other, and there is one breath to all. What has the man more than the animal? Nothing, for all, is vanity. All go to one place. All were formed of the dust, and all will return to dust. Who has seen the spirit of the sons of man, whether it goes upward? Or the spirit of the beast, whether it goes down into the land?[2] I saw that there was no good. That in which a man rejoices from his works, is just his joy, for who will take him to see anything of that which will be after him?"

Ecclesiastes: Chapter 3 Notes

1 Codex Vaticanus: ouranon (ΟΥΡΑΝΟΝ). Translation: sky (or Uranus)

- Aleppo Codex: šmym (שמים). Translation: skies (or Shamayim)

- Leningrad Codex: shamayim (שָׁמָיִם). Translation: skies (or Shamayim)

- Targum to Ecclesiastes: šemayyā (שְׁמַיָּא). Translation: skies

2 Codex Vaticanus: gên (ΓΗΝ). Translation: land (or Ge, Gaia)

- Aleppo Codex: årṣ (ארץ). Translation: land (or Eretz)

- Leningrad Codex: aretz (אֶרֶץ). Translation: land (or Eretz)

- Targum to Ecclesiastes: arôā (אַרְעָא). Translation: land

Ecclesiastes: Chapter 4

"So I returned, and saw all the oppression that was done under the sun, and saw the tears of the oppressed, and they had no comforter. On the side of those that oppressed them was power, and they had no comforter. I praised all the dead that had already died more than the living, as many as have lived until now. Even better than both of these is he who has not yet been born; who has not seen all the evil work that is done under the Sun. I saw all labor, and all the diligent work, that this is a man's envy from his neighbor. This is also vanity and waywardness of spirit. The fool works with his hands and eats his own flesh. Better is a handful of rest than two handfuls of trouble and waywardness of spirit."

"So I returned and saw vanity under the Sun. There is one alone, and there is not a second. Yes, he has neither son nor brother, yet there is no end to all his labor. Neither are his eyes satisfied with wealth. For whom do I labor, and deprive my mind of good? This is also vanity and evil trouble."

"Two are better than one, seeing they have a good reward for their labor. For if they fall, the one will lift his fellow, but woe to him that is alone when he falls, as there is not a second to lift him up. Also, if two should lie together they get heat, but how will one be warmed alone? If one should prevail against him, the two will withstand him, and a threefold cord will not be quickly broken."

"Better is a poor and wise child than an old and senile king, who does not know how to concentrate any longer. He will come out of the house of the prisoners to reign because he also that was in his kingdom has become poor."

"I saw all the living who were walking under the Sun, with the youths who will stand up in each one's place. There is no end to all the people, to all who were before them, and the last will not rejoice in them, for this also is vanity and waywardness of spirit."

"Keep walking, whenever you go to the Temple of God.[1] When you are near enough to hear, let your sacrifice be better than the gift of fools, for they don't know that they are doing evil."

Ecclesiastes: Chapter 4 Notes

1 Codex Vaticanus: oecon tou theou (ΟΙΚΟΝΤΟΥΘΕΟΥ). Translation: temple of the god

• Aleppo Codex: byt hålhym (בית האלהים). Translation: house of the god

• Leningrad Codex: beit ha'elohim (בֵּית הָאֱלֹהִים). Translation: house of the god

• Targum to Ecclesiastes: mûqedešā dayāy (מוּקְדְּשָׁא דַיְיָ).
Translation: temple of Yhů

Ecclesiastes: Chapter 5

"Do not be quick with your mouth, and don't let your heart be swift to say anything before God, for God is in the sky above, and you are on Earth. Therefore, let your words be few. Through a multitude of trials, a dream comes, and a fool's voice is with a multitude of words. Whenever you make a vow to God, don't forget to pay it for he takes no pleasure in fools. Pay, therefore, whatever you have vowed. It is better that you should not vow than that you should vow and not pay. Don't allow your mouth to lead your flesh to sin, and don't say in the presence of God, 'It was a mistake,' in case God becomes angry at your words, and destroys the works of your hands. There is evil in a multitude of dreams and vanities and many words, but fear God."

"If you should see the oppression of the poor, and the wresting of judgment and justice in the land, don't wonder at the matter, for there is a high one to watch over him that is high and high ones over them. Also, the abundance of the Earth is for everyone. The king is dependent on the farmed fields. He who loves silver will not be satisfied with silver. Whoever has loved gain, and the abundance of it, this is also vanity."

"In the multitude of good, they are increased who eat it, and what virtue has the owner, but the right of seeing it with his eyes? The sleep of a slave is sweet, whether he eats little or much, but to one who is satiated with wealth, none allow him to sleep."

"There is an infirmity which I have seen under the Sun, namely, wealth kept for its owner to his pain. That wealth will perish evilly, and the man begets a son, and there is nothing in his hand. As he came forth naked from his mother's womb, he will return back as he came, and he will receive nothing for his labor, that it should go with him in his hand. This is also an evil infirmity, for as he came, so also will he return, and what is his gain, for which he vainly works? Yes, all his days are in darkness, mourning, great sorrow, infirmity, and anger."

"Look, I have seen good, that it is a fine thing for a man to eat and to drink, and to see good in all his labor that he may work under the Sun, all the number of the days of his life which God has given to him, for it is his portion. Yes, and as for every man to whom God has given wealth and possessions, and has given him the power to eat, and to receive his portion, and to rejoice in his labor, this is the gift of God. For he will not remember the days of his life, for God troubles him in the joy of his heart."

Ecclesiastes: Chapter 6

"There is an evil which I have seen under the Sun, and it is plentiful among men. A man to whom God will give wealth, and substance, and honor, and he lacks nothing for his mind from all things that he will desire, yet God will not give him the power to eat it, as a stranger will devour it. This is vanity and an evil infirmity."

"If a man fathers a hundred children, and lives many years, however many the days of his years will be, yet, his mind is not satisfied with good, then he has no burial. I said, 'An untimely birth is better than his, for he came in vanity, and departs in darkness, and his name will be covered in darkness. Moreover, he has not seen the Sun, nor known rest. There is no more rest for this one than another. Though he has lived to see a thousand years, yet he has seen no good.' Do not all go to the same place?"

"All the labor of a man is for his mouth, and yet the appetite will not be satisfied. For what advantage has the wise man over the fool, since even the poor knows how to walk in the direction of life? The sight of the eyes is better than that which wanders in the mind, this is also vanity, and waywardness of spirit. If anything has been, its name has already been called, and it is known what man is. He cannot contend with him who is stronger than he, for there are many things which increase vanity."

Ecclesiastes: Chapter 7

"What advantage has a man? Who knows what is good for a man in his life, during the number of days of his life of vanity? He has spent them like a shadow, for who will tell a man what will be after him under the Sun? A good name is better than good oil, and the day of death than the day of birth. It is better to go to the house of mourning than to go to the banquet house, since this is the end of every man, and the living man will apply good warning to his heart. Sorrow is better than laughter, for by the sadness of the countenance the heart will be made better. The heart of the wise is in the house of mourning, but the heart of fools is in the house of humor. It is better to hear a reproof of a wise man than for a man to hear the song of fools. As the sound of thorns under a cauldron, so is the laughter of fools. This is also vanity."

"Oppression makes a wise man mad and destroys his noble heart. The end of a matter is better than the beginning of it. The patient is better than the high-minded. Do not be quick in your spirit to become angry, for anger will lodge in the chest of fools."

"Don't say, 'What has happened, that the previous times were better than these? You do not inquire wisely concerning this. Wisdom is good with an inheritance, and there is an advantage by it to those who see the Sun.

For wisdom in its shadow is as the shadow of silver, and the excellence of the knowledge of wisdom will give life to he who has it."

"See the works of God, for who will be able to straighten him who God has made crooked? In the day of prosperity live joyfully, and consider in the day of adversity. Consider, I say, God also has caused the one to agree with the other for this reason, that man should find nothing after him. I have seen all things in the days of my vanity, and a just man is perishing in his justice, and an ungodly man is remaining in his wickedness. Do not be very just, nor be very wise, in case you are confused. Do not be very wicked, and do not be stubborn, in case you should die before your time. It is good for you to hold fast to this, also by this: don't defile your hands, for to them that fear God all things will come out well."

"Wisdom will help the wise man more than ten mighty men which are in the city. For there is not a righteous man in the earth, who will only do good and never sin. Also pay no attention to all the words that ungodly men will speak, in case you hear your servant cursing you. For many times he will trespass against you, and repeatedly will he afflict your heart, for you have also cursed others the same way."

"All these things I have proved in wisdom. I said, 'I will be wise,' but it was far from me. That which is far away, and at a great depth, who will learn about? I and my heart went around to know, and to examine, and to seek wisdom, and the account of things, and to know the foolishness and trouble and madness of the ungodly man."

"I find her to be, I will say, more bitter than death, the woman which is a trap, and her heart like nets, she who has a band in her hands. He that is good in the sight of God will be delivered from her, but the sinner will be caught by her. 'Look, this I have learned,' said the apostle, 'Searching one at a time to find out, which my mind searched for but I did not find, for I have found one man in a thousand, but among women in all these I have not found any. But, look, this I have learned, that God made man upright, but they have searched out many devices."

Ecclesiastes: Chapter 8

"Who knows the wise, and who knows the interpretation of a saying? A man's wisdom will lighten his attitude, but a man of shameless attitude will be hated. Follow the commandment of the king, because of the words of the oath of God. Do not be quick to leave his presence. Do not partake in evil, for he will do whatever he pleases like a king who has the power, and who will ask him, 'What are you doing?'"

He who keeps the commandment will not know an evil thing, and the heart of the wise knows the time of judgment. For everything, there is time and judgment. The knowledge of a man is great to him. For there is no one that knows what is going to be. Who will tell him how it will be? No man has power over the spirit to detain it, and there is no power over the day of death. There is no discharge in the day of the battle, nor will ungodliness save a devotee."

"So I saw all this, and I applied my heart to every work that has been done under the Sun. All the things in which man has power over man to afflict him. Then I saw the ungodly carried into the tombs, and that out of the holy place they departed and were praised in the city because they had done this. This also is vanity, because there is no contradiction made on the part of those who do evil quickly, therefore the heart of the children of men is fully determined in them to do evil."

"He who has sinned has done evil from that time, and long before. Nevertheless I know that it is good for those who fear God, but it will not be good for the ungodly. He will not prolong his days, which are like a shadow because he does not fear God."

"There is vanity which is done on the Earth, that there are righteous people for which it happens according as should happen to the ungodly, and there are ungodly men for which happens as it should for the just. I said, 'This is also vanity.' Then I praised humor, because there is no good for a man under the Sun, but to eat, and drink, and be merry, and this will keep him in his labor all the days of his life, which God has given him under the sun."

"Then I set my heart to know wisdom and to perceive the trouble that was worked on the Earth, for there are those that neither by day nor night sees sleep with his eyes. I saw all the works of God, that a man will not be able to discover the work which is worked under the Sun. Whatever things a man will endeavor to seek, however, a man may labor to seek it, he will not find it. However much a wise man may speak of knowing it, he will not be able to find it, for I applied all this to my heart, and my heart has seen all this."

Ecclesiastes: Chapter 9

"Who knows the wise, and who knows the interpretation of a saying? A man's wisdom will lighten his attitude, but a man of shameless attitude will be hated. Follow the commandment of the king, because of the words of the oath of God. Do not be quick to leave his presence. Do not partake in evil, for he will do whatever he pleases like a king who has the power, and who will ask him, 'What are you doing?'"

He who keeps the commandment will not know an evil thing, and the heart of the wise knows the time of judgment. For everything, there is time and judgment. The knowledge of a man is great to him. For there is no one that knows what is going to be. Who will tell him how it will be? No man has power over the spirit to detain it, and there is no power over the day of death. There is no discharge in the day of the battle, nor will ungodliness save a devotee."

"So I saw all this, and I applied my heart to every work that has been done under the Sun. All the things in which man has power over man to afflict him. Then I saw the ungodly carried into the tombs, and that out of the holy place they departed and were praised in the city because they had done this. This also is vanity, because there is no contradiction made on the part of those who do evil quickly, therefore the heart of the children of men is fully determined in them to do evil."

"He who has sinned has done evil from that time, and long before. Nevertheless I know that it is good for those who fear God, but it will not be good for the ungodly. He will not prolong his days, which are like a shadow because he does not fear God."

"There is vanity which is done on the Earth, that there are righteous people for which it happens according as should happen to the ungodly, and there are ungodly men for which happens as it should for the just. I said, 'This is also vanity.' Then I praised humor, because there is no good for a man under the Sun, but to eat, and drink, and be merry, and this will keep him in his labor all the days of his life, which God has given him under the sun."

"Then I set my heart to know wisdom and to perceive the trouble that was worked on the Earth, for there are those that neither by day nor night sees sleep with his eyes. I saw all the works of God, that a man will not be able to discover the work which is worked under the Sun. Whatever things a man will endeavor to seek, however, a man may labor to seek it, he will not find it. However much a wise man may speak of knowing it, he will not be able to find it, for I applied all this to my heart, and my heart has seen all this."

Ecclesiastes: Chapter 10

"Pestilent flies will corrupt a prepared sweet ointment, and a little wisdom is more precious than great glory of foolishness."

"A wise man's heart is at his right hand, but a fool's heart is at his left. Yes, and whenever a fool walks by the way, his heart will fail him, and all that he thinks of is foolishness. If the spirit of the ruler rises against you, don't leave your place, for soothing will put an end to great offenses."

"There is an evil which I have seen under the Sun, in which an error has come from the ruler, and the fools have been set in very high places, while rich men sit in low ones. I have seen servants on horses, and princes walking like servants on the earth."

"He that digs a pit will fall into it, and he that breaks down a hedge will be bitten by a serpent. He that removes stones will be troubled by it, and he that chops wood will be endangered by it. If the ax head should fall off, then the man troubles his attitude, and he must put out more strength, and in that case, skill is of no advantage to a man. If a serpent bites when there is no charmer's whisper, then there is no advantage to the charmer. The words of a wise mouth are gracious, but the lips of a fool will swallow him up. The beginning of the words in his mouth is foolishness and the end of his talk is mischievous madness. A fool moreover multiplies words. Man does not know what has been, or what will be. Who will tell him what will come after him? The labor of fools will afflict them, like that of one who doesn't know to go to the city."

"Woe to you, a city whose king is young, and your princes eat in the morning! Blessed are you, land, whose king is a son of nobles, and whose princes will eat seasonably, for strength, and will not be ashamed. By slothful neglect, a building will be brought low, and by the idleness of the hands, the house will fall to pieces. Men prepare bread for laughter, and wine and oil that the living should rejoice, but to money, all things will humbly yield obedience. Even in your conscience, don't curse the king, and don't curse the rich in your bedchamber, for a bird of the air will carry your voice, and that which has wings will report your speech."

Ecclesiastes: Chapter 11

"Send out your bread on the face of the water, for you will find it after many days. Give a portion to seven, and also to eight, for you don't know what evil there will be on the Earth. If the clouds are filled with rain, they pour it out on the Earth, and whether a tree falls southward or northward, in the place where the tree falls, there it will be. He that observes the wind doesn't sow, and he that watches at the clouds will not reap. Among those, who knows which way the wind is blowing? Like how the bones are hidden in the womb of a pregnant woman, likewise you will not know the works of God, even all things that he will do."

"In the morning sow your seed, and in the evening don't let your hand be idle, for you don't know what sort will prosper, whether this or that, or whether both will be good alike. Moreover, the light is sweet, and it is good for the eyes to see the Sun. Even if a man should live many years, and rejoice in them all, let him remember the days of darkness, for they will be many. All that comes is vanity."

"Rejoice, young man, in your youth, and let your heart cheer you in the days of your youth, and walk in the ways of your heart blameless, but not in the sight of your eyes. Yet, know that for all these things God will judge you. Therefore remove sorrow from your heart, and put away evil from your flesh, for youth and foolish-ness are vanity."

Ecclesiastes: Chapter 12

"Remember your creator in the days of your youth, before the days of evil come, and the years overtake you in which you will say, 'I have no pleasure in them.' While the Sun and light[1] are not yet darkened, nor the moon and the stars, nor the clouds returning after the rain, in the day in which the keepers of the house will tremble and the mighty men will become bent, and the grinding women cease because they have become few. The women looking out the windows into the dark will shut the doors in the marketplace, because of the weakness of the voice of her who grinds at the mill. He will rise at the voice of the sparrow, and all the daughters of song will be brought down. They will look up, and fears will be in the way. The almond tree will blossom, and the locust will increase, and the caper will be scattered, because man has gone to his eternal home, and the mourners have gone around the market."

"Before the silver cord is let go, or the best gold is broken, or the pitcher be broken at the fountain, or the wheel run down to the cistern. Before the dust also returns to the earth as it was, and the spirit returns to God who gave it. Vanity of vanities," said the apostle, "all is vanity."

Because the apostle was wise above others, he taught man excellent knowledge, and the ear will trace out the parables. The apostle searched diligently to find out acceptable words, and correct writing, even words of truth. The words of the wise are like whips, and like nails firmly fastened, which have been given from one shepherd by agreement. Moreover, my son, guard yourself using them, of making many books there is no end, and much study is a weariness of the flesh. Hear the end of the matter, the Sun. Fear God, and keep his commandments, for this is the whole man. For God will bring every work into judgment everything that has been overlooked, whether it is good, or whether it is evil.

Ecclesiastes: Chapter 12 Notes

1 Codex Vaticanus: êlios cae to phôs (ⲎⲀⲒⲞⲤⲔⲀⲒⲦⲞⲫⲰⲤ). Translation: sun (or Helios) and the light

• Aleppo Codex: hšmš ûhåûr (השמש והאור). Translation: the sun (or Shemesh) and the light (or fire)

• Leningrad Codex: hashemesh veha'or (הַשֶּׁמֶשׁ וְהָאֹור). Translation: the sun (or Shemesh) and the light (or fire)

• Targum to Ecclesiastes: lešimšā ûnehôrā (לְשִׁמְשָׁא וּנְהֹורָא). Translation: the sun and the light

During the Bronze Age, the "light" was the region around the sun that rose before the sun each morning, and set after the sun each evening. The Egyptians interpreted this as the Hathor, the "house of Horus," most of the time. During the Amarna Period, the "light" was interpreted as Aten, which became the supreme god. The "light" never appears to have been viewed as particularly important by the Israelites and other Canaanites.

Song of Songs: Chapter 1

The Song of songs, which is about Solomon.

Let him kiss me with the kisses of his mouth.

Your breasts are better than wine. The smell of your ointments is better than all spices, your name is ointment poured out, and therefore the young maidens love you. They have drawn you, and we will run after you, for the smell of your ointments.

The king has brought me into the treasury, and let us rejoice and be glad in you.

We will love your breasts more than wine, and right-eousness loves you.

I am black[1] but beautiful you daughters of Jerusalem, like the tents of Qedar[2] and like the curtains of Solomon. Don't view me thinking I am dark because the sun has looked unfavorably on me.

My mother's sons struggled with me, and they made me keeper in the vineyards, but I have not kept my own vineyard. Tell me, you who my mind loves, where you tend your flock, and where you cause them to rest at noon, so I can become like one that is veiled by the flocks surrounding you. If you don't know yourself, you are beautiful to women, go out by the path of the flocks, and feed your kids by the shepherd's tents. I have compared you, my companion, to my horses and the chariots of Pharaoh. How are your cheeks beautiful as those of a dove, your neck like chains! We will make you figures of gold with studs of silver.

So long as the king was at my table, my spikenard[3] gave out its odor. My beloved[4] is to me a like bundle of myrrh, and he will lie between my breasts. My beloved is to me like the Ambrosia from Cyprus,[5] in the vineyards of Ein Gedi.[6] Look, you are fair, my companion, look, you are fair, your eyes are doves. Look, you are fair, my beloved, yes, beautiful, overshadowing our bed. The beams of our house are cedars, our ceilings are of cypress.

Song of Songs: Chapter 1 Notes

1 Codex Vaticanus: melaena (ΜΕΛΑΙΝΑ). Translation: black (or dark-skinned)

• Dead Sea Scroll 6QCantᵃ: š-ḥrt (ש-חרת). Dead Sea Scroll 6QCantᵃ is damaged in the middle of the word, however, it does appear to b the same word.

• Aleppo Codex: šḥrḥrt (שחרחרת). Translation: feminine dark (or swarthy)

• Leningrad Codex: shecharchoret (שְׁחַרְחֹרֶת). Translation: feminine dark (or swarthy)

• Targum to Song of Songs: qadrîtā (קַדְרִיתָא). Translation: black (or miserable)

This statement appears to be identical to the modern usage of the term 'black' to denote people of very dark skin color. According to the Torah, many Egyptians and Kushites left Egypt with Moses and the Israelites, and integrated into the twelve tribes. Moses' second wife was described as being a Kushite. The Kushites were people from Kush, a Nubian kingdom south of Egypt which had been conquered by the Egyptians. Nubians were, and still are a dark-skinned people.

Additionally, a large number of Nubians served within the Egyptian armies of Thutmose III, who conquered Canaan circa 1450 BC. The records of Egypt's conquest specifically mention the town of Shunaam being conquered, which is later mentioned in this Song, supporting the idea that this woman was in fact dark-skinned.

2 Codex Vaticanus: Cêdar (ⲔⲎⲆⲀⲢ)

- Aleppo Codex: qdr (קדר)
- Leningrad Codex: kedar (קֵדָ֔ר)
- Targum to Song of Songs: qēdār (קְדָר)

The Qedarites were a nomadic tribe of Arabs who lived east of Canaan during the Neo-Assyrian Empire, in the 8th and 7th centuries BC. It is unclear where they were living prior to that, and is believed they were absorbed into the Nabataean culture by the 2nd century AD. In Islam, the prophet Mohammad is believed to have been a descendant of the Qedarites.

3 Codex Vaticanus: nardos (ⲚⲀⲢⲆⲞⲤ). Translation: spikenard

- Aleppo Codex: nrd (נרד). Translation: spikenard
- Leningrad Codex: nirdi (נְרְדְּ). Translation: spikenard
- Targum to Song of Songs: nirdā (נִרְדָּא). Translation: spikenard

Spikenard, also called nard or muskroot, is a plant that grows in the Himalayas, in India, Nepal, and China. Oils made from it were widely traded throughout the ancient world, as far west as the Roman Empire. It was used to make perfumes and medicine, as well as in religious ceremonies.

4 Codex Vaticanus: adelphidos (ΑΕΛΦΙΔΟϹ). Translation: fraternal brother

- Aleppo Codex: dŭd (דוד). Translation: uncle (or David, beloved)
- Leningrad Codex: dôdi (דּוֹדִי). Translation: uncle (or David, beloved)
- Targum to Song of Songs: dāwid (דּוִד). Translation: David

In ancient Greek usage "brother" was not limited to biological brothers, but any close male friend was considered a brother. In the Hebrew society, men would marry teenage "women," resulting in the word "uncle" being used by girls and women in a similar fashion to the Greek usage of "brother." In the Hebrew context "uncle" could be interpreted as "beloved male" or "male lover."

5 Codex Vaticanus: botrys tês cyprou (ΒΟΤΡΥϹ ΤΗϹ ΚΥΠΡΟΥ). Translation: ambrosia (or unripened grapes, Pleiades) from Cyprus

- Aleppo Codex: kpr (כפר). Translation: village (or tomb)
- Leningrad Codex: kōper (כֹּפֶר). Translation: village (or tomb)
- Targum to Song of Songs: kappar (כַּפֵּר). Translation: village (or tomb)

The exact translation of this verse has been debated for thousands for years. The meaning of the Hebrew kpr (כפר) is not clear in this context, and it is theorized to be a scribal error of qmpůr (קמפור), however, this would be a significant anachronism, as Camphor was introduced to the Middle East and Europe during the Islamic era. It is also sometimes viewed as a scribal error for the word kůpr (כּוֹפֶר), which means henna, which has been used in the region since at least the Bronze Age. This "spelling error" appears to be an older spelling of the word, as the Canaanite spelling was kpr (𐎋𐎔𐎗) in Ugaritic script, and then kpr (𐤊𐤐𐤓) in Phoenician script. This spelling indicates that the Hebrew Song of Songs was translated from a Phoenician source text.

The Greek translators could not have translated kpr (𐤊𐤐𐤓) as "ambrosia from Cyprus," suggesting the Aramaic version of Song of Songs read bśrå kůprå (עֲנַבְיָא עֲנַבְיָא), meaning "unrippened grape smear," which was then misinterpreted by the Greek translators. The Aramaic word bůsrå (עֲנַבְיָא), or an earlier Phoenician variant used in Cyprus, is believed to be the origin of the Greek word botrys (βότρυς), meaning both "ambrosia" and "unrippened grape." The original term used in the text appear to be a reference to the anti-aging skin ointment used in ancient Egypt, which was made from unripened grapes. The ointment was rich in arsenic, which seems to be the cause of many of the deaths of the Egyptian nobility that could afford it, however, would have also been rich in anti-oxidents, making the users' skin appear younger.

6 Codex Vaticanus: Engaddi (ϵⲚⲅⲁⲇⲇⲓ).
- Aleppo Codex: ôyn gdy (עֵין גְדִי)
- Leningrad Codex: ein gedi (עֵין גֶּדִי)
- Targum to Song of Songs: ên gedî (עֵין גֶּדִי)

Ein Gedi is an oasis in modern Israel west of the Dead Sea. This note was added to the Septuagint when it was translated.

Song of Songs: Chapter 2

I am a flower of the plain, a lily of the valleys. As a lily among thorns, so is my companion among the daughters. As the apple among the trees of the wood, so is my beloved among the sons. I desired his shadow and sat down, and his fruit was sweet in my throat. Bring me into the wine house, and set love before me. Strengthen me with perfumes, stay me with apples, for I am wounded with love. His left hand will be under my head, and his right hand will embrace me. I have cursed you, you daughters of Jerusalem, by Sabatoh and the powerful demons, so you do not arouse or wake my love until he pleases.

The voice of my beloved! See, he comes leaping over the mountains, bounding over the hills. My beloved is like a roe or a young hart on the mountains of Bethel, see, he is behind our wall, looking through the windows, peeping through the lattices.

My beloved answers, and says to me, "Rise, come, my companion, my fair one, my dove. For, look, the winter is past, the rain is gone, it has departed. The flowers are seen in the land, and the time of pruning has arrived, and the voice of the turtle-dove has been heard in our land. The fig tree has put out its young figs, the vines put out the tender grape, and they yield a smell. Rise, come, my companion, my fair one, my dove, and yes, come. You are my dove, in the shelter of the rock, near the wall. Show me your face, and cause me to hear your voice, for your voice is sweet, and your countenance is beautiful. Bring us the little foxes that spoil the vines, for our vines put out tender grapes."

My beloved is mine, and I am his, he feeds his flock among the lilies. Until the day dawn, and the shadows leave, turn, my beloved, be like a roe, or young deer on the mountains of the ravines.

Song of Songs: Chapter 2 Notes

1 Codex Vaticanus: en taes dynamesin cae en taes ischysesin tou agrou (ЄN ΤΑΙϹ ΔΥΝΑΜЄϹΙΝ ΚΑΙ ЄN ΤΑΙϹ ΙϹΧΥϹЄϹΙΝ ΤΟΥ ΑΓΡΟΥ). Translation: in (or into) the forces and in (or into) the powerful (or potent) the field (or land)

• Aleppo Codex: bṣbåůt åů båylůt hšdh (**בצבאות או באילות השדה**). Translation: in (or at, with) militaries (or Sabaoth) or (or either) in (or at, with) stag (or male deer) the field (or female demon)

• Leningrad Codex: bitzva'ot o be'aylotha sadeh (אֹו בִּצְבָאֹות בְּאַיְלֹותַ֥ הַשָּׂדֶ֑ה). Translation: in (or at, with) militaries (or Sabaoth) or (or either) in (or at, with) stag (or male deer) the field (or female demon, Aramaic: Shaddai)

• Targum to Song of Songs: bayāy sebāôt ûbetaqqîpê arā (בְּיָי צְבָאֹות וּבְתַקִּיפֵי אַרְעָא). Translation: the Yhů militaries and in attack land

The Greek and Hebrew texts are similar, while the Aramaic Targum has the phrase in the middle of a large unrelated paragraph. The Greek text appears to be a translation of the Aramaic "in Sabaoth and the powerful demons," which is used as a translation. The Aramaic translation was probably fairly recent when the Greek translation was made. It's likely that an earlier Canaanite version of the text would have read "in Shaddai and the powerful Adama," before Sabaoth replaced Shaddai. Adama was a southern Canaanite goddess of the underworld and wife of Shaddai, the late Bronze Age reinterpretation of Reshef in southern Canaan.

Song of Songs: Chapter 3

By night on my bed, I wanted him who my mind loves. I wanted him but did not find him. I called him, but he did not hear me. I will rise now, and go around the city, in the marketplaces, and the streets, and I will seek he who my mind loves. I searched for him, but I did not find him. The watchmen who go their rounds in the city found me.

I asked, "Have you seen he who my mind loves?"

A little while after I left them, I found he who my mind loves, and I held him and did not let him go, until I brought him into my mother's house, and into the room of she that conceived me. I have ordered you, "Daughters of Jerusalem, by the powers and by the virtues of the field, that you did not rouse or awake my love until he pleases. Who is this that comes up from the wilderness like pillars of smoke, perfumed with myrrh and frankincense, with all powders of the perfumer?"

Look at Solomon's bed. Sixty strong men of the mighty ones of Israel are around it. They each held a sword, being experts in war. Every man had his sword on his thigh because of fear at night. King Solomon made himself a bed of wood from Lebanon. He made its pillars from silver, its bottom from gold, and its covering from scarlet, and under it a pavement of love for the daughters of Jerusalem. Go out, you daughters of Zion, and see

King Solomon, with the crown where his mother crowned him, on the day of his marriage, and the day of the celebration of his heart.

Song of Songs: Chapter 4

Look, you are beautiful, my companion. Look, you are fair. Your eyes are doves, next to your veil. Your hair is like the flocks of goats, that have appeared from Gilead. Your teeth are as flocks of shorn sheep, that have been washed, all of them bearing twins, and there is not a barren one among them. Your lips are like a thread of scarlet, and your speech is beautiful like the rind of a pomegranate is your cheek without your veil. Your neck is like the tower of David, that was built as an armory, a thousand shields hang on it, and all darts of mighty men. Your two breasts are like two twin fawns, that feed among the lilies. Until the day dawns, and the shadows leave, I will take myself to the mountain of myrrh, and the hill of frankincense.

You are all fair, my companion, and there is no spot in you. Come from Lebanon, my bride, come from Lebanon, and you will come and pass from the beginning of faith, from the peaks of Senir[1] and Hermon,[2] from the lions' dens, from the mountains of the leopards. My sister, my spouse, you have ravished my heart, and you have ravished my heart with one of your eyes, with one chain of your neck.

How beautiful are your breasts, my sister, my spouse! How much more beautiful are your breasts than wine, and the smell of your garments than all spices! Your lips drop honeycomb, my spouse, honey and milk are under your tongue, and the smell of your garments is as the smell of Lebanon. My sister, my spouse is a garden enclosed, a garden enclosed, a fountain sealed. Your shoots are a garden of pomegranates, with the fruit of best fruit-trees of Cyprus, with spikenard, spikenard and saffron, calamus and cinnamon, with all woods of Lebanon, myrrh, aloe, with all chief spices, a fountain of a garden, and a well of water springing and gurgling from Lebanon. Awake, north wind, and come, south and blow through my garden, and let my spices flow out.

Song of Songs: Chapter 4 Notes

1 Codex Vaticanus: Sanir (ᴄᴀɴɪᵖ)

- Aleppo Codex: Šnyr (שניר)

- Leningrad Codex: Senir (שְׂנִיר)

- Targum to Song of Songs: tûr talgā (טוּר תַּלְגָּא). Translation: mountain of snow

Mount Senir is a prominent mountain in the Anti-Lebanon mountains in northern modern Israel. Dead Sea Scroll 4QCant[b] contained a shorted verse here, not mentioning Mount Senir. Dead Sea Scroll 4QCant[b] is dated to the Herodian Dynasty (37 BC to 6 AD).

2 Codex Vaticanus: Ermôn (ϵᴘᴍⲱɴ)

- Dead Sea Scroll 4QCant[b]: Åŭmnŭn (אוֹמנוֹן)

- Aleppo Codex: hrmŭn (חרמון)

- Leningrad Codex: ḥermôn (חֶרְמֹוֹן)
- Targum to Song of Songs: ḥermôn (חֶרְמֹון)

Mount Hermon is a prominent mountain in the Anti-Lebanon mountains in northern modern Israel, southwest Syria, and southeast Lebanon, with a UN Buffer Zone between them. In the Hebrew Book of Enoch (1st Enoch), Mount Hermon was the place where the watchers descended from the sky before taking human wives. Dead Sea Scroll 4QCant[a] appears to have never included the end of chapter 4, chapter 5, and the beginning of chapter 6. Dead Sea Scroll 4QCant[b] contained a shorted verse here, and it is not clear if Åůmnůn was a corruption of Hermon, or if it was an alternate spelling of Amnon (אַמְנֹון), the oldest son of King David. It is unlikely that a song about King Solomon would mention Amnon, and Solomon did have a palace on Mount Hermon, supporting the term Hermon being in the original version of the verse. Dead Sea Scroll 4QCant[b] is dated to the Herodian Dynasty (37 BC to 6 AD).

Song of Songs: Chapter 5

Let my beloved come down into his garden, and eat the fruit of his choice berries. I have come into my garden, my sister, my spouse. I have gathered my myrrh with my spices. I have eaten my bread with my honey, and I have drunk my wine with my milk. Eat, my friends, and drink! Yes, brothers, drink abundantly. I sleep, but my heart is awake, and the voice of my beloved knocks at the door, saying, "Open. open to me, my companion, my sister, my dove, my perfect one, for my head is filled with dew, and my hair with the drops of the night. I have taken off my coat, and how will I put it on? I have washed my feet, how will I defile them?"

My beloved put out his hand by the hole of the door, and my belly moved for him. I rose up to open to my beloved, my hands dropped myrrh, my fingers smeared myrrh, on the handles of the lock. I opened to my beloved, and my beloved was gone. My mind[1] failed at his speech, and I wanted him but did not find him. I called him, but he did not answer me. The watchman that went on their rounds in the city found me, and they struck me and wounded me. The keepers of the walls took away my veil. I have cursed you, daughters of Jerusalem, by Sabaoth and the powerful demons, if you should find my beloved, what are you to say to him? That I am wounded with love.

Who is your beloved to be more than another beloved, you beautiful among women? Who is your beloved, to be more than another beloved, that you have so ordered us?

"My beloved is white and ruddy, chosen out from tens of thousands. His head is like very fine gold, his locks are flowing, black as a raven. His eyes are as doves, by the pools of waters, washed with milk, sitting by the pools. His cheeks are as bowls of spices pouring out perfumes, his lips are lilies, dropping choice myrrh. His hands are as turned gold set with beryl, his belly is an ivory tablet on a sapphire stone. His legs are marble pillars set on golden sockets, his form is like Lebanon, choice as the cedars. His throat is most sweet, and altogether desirable. This is my beloved, and this is my companion, daughters of Jerusalem."

"Where has your beloved gone, you beautiful among women? Where has your beloved turned aside? Tell us, and we will seek him for you."

Song of Songs: Chapter 5 Notes

1 Codex Vaticanus: psychê (𐤕𐤅𐤗𐤄). Translation: mind (or personality, psyche)

• Aleppo Codex: npš (𐤅𐤔𐤄). Translation: mind (or life, soul, person)

- Leningrad Codex: nafshi (נַפְשִׁ). Translation: mind (or life, soul, person)
- Targum to Song of Songs: napši (נַפְּשִׁ). Translation: mind (or life, soul, person)

Dead Sea Scroll 4QCant[a] appears to have never included the end of chapter 4, chapter 5, and the beginning of chapter 6. Dead Sea Scroll 4QCant[a] is dated to the Herodian Dynasty (37 BC to 6 AD).

Song of Songs: Chapter 6

My beloved is gone down to his garden, to the beds of spice, to feed his flock in the gardens, and to gather lilies. I am my beloved's, and my beloved is mine, who feeds among the lilies. You are beautiful, my companion, like pleasure,[1] beautiful as Jerusalem, and terrible as armies set in formation. Turn away your eyes from before me, for they have ravished me. Your hair is as flocks of goats that have appeared from Gilead. Your teeth are as flocks of shorn sheep, that have just been washed, all of them bearing twins, and there is none barren among them. Your lips are like a thread of scarlet, and your speech is beautiful. Your cheek is like the rind of a pomegranate, being seen without your veil.

There are sixty queens, and eighty concubines, and maidens without number. My dove, my perfect one is one, she is the only one of her mother, and she is the choice of her that gave birth to her. The daughters saw her, and the queens will pronounce her blessed, yes, and the concubines, and they will praise her. Who is this that looks out like the morning, beautiful as the moon, choice as the sun, terrible as armies set in formation?

I went down to the garden of nuts, to look at the fruits of the valley, to see if the vine flowered if the pomegranates blossomed. There I will give you my breasts, but my mind did not know it.

Song of Songs: Chapter 6 Notes

1 Codex Vaticanus: eudocia (ⲈⲨⲆⲞⲔⲒⲀ), Translation: good (or pleasure)

- Aleppo Codex: trṣh (תרצה). Translation: to please

- Leningrad Codex: tirṣâ (תִּרְצָה). Translation: to please

Dead Sea Scroll 4QCantᵃ appears to have never included the end of chapter 4, chapter 5, and the beginning of chapter 6. Dead Sea Scroll 4QCantᵃ is dated to the Herodian Dynasty (37 BC to 6 AD).

Song of Songs: Chapter 7

It made me like the chariots of Abinadab. Return, return, Shulamite.[1] Return, return, and we will look at you. What will you see in the Shulamite? She comes like bands of armies. Your steps are beautiful in shoes, daughter of the prince, the joints of your thighs are like chains, the work of the craftsman. Your navel is as a turned bowl, not lacking liquor, your belly is as a heap of wheat set about with lilies. Your two breasts are like two twin fawns. Your neck is like an ivory tower, and your eyes are like pools in Heshbon, by the gates of the daughter of many, your nose is like the tower of Lebanon, looking towards Damascus. Your head is like Carmel,[2] and the curls of your hair like scarlet. The king is bound in the galleries. How beautiful are you, and how sweet are you, my love? This is your greatness in your delights, you were made like a palm tree, and your chest a cluster.

I said, "I will go up to the palm tree, and I will take hold of its high boughs. Now your breasts will be like clusters of the vine, and your odor like apples, and your throat like good wine, going well with my beloved, suiting my lips and teeth. I am my beloved's, and his desire is towards me. Come, my beloved, let us go out into the field, let us lodge in the villages. Let us go early into the vineyards, let us see if the vine has flowered and if the blossoms have appeared, if the pomegranates have blossomed there, I will give you my breasts. The mandrakes have given a smell, and at our doors are all kinds of choice fruits, new and old. My beloved, I have kept them for you."

Song of Songs: Chapter 7 Notes

1 Codex Vaticanus: Soulamitis (ϹΟΥΛΑΜΙΤΙϹ)

• Aleppo Codex: Šŭlmyt (שׁוּלמית). Translation: Shulammitess

• Leningrad Codex: Shulammit (שׁוּלַמִּית). Translation: Shulammitess

The term Shulamite refers to people from the town of Shunaam, which was located near the Jezreel Valley, north of Mount Gilboa, in the tribal lands of Issachar at the time. The town of Shunaam was listed as one of the towns conquered by the Egyptian Pharaoh Thutmose III circa 1450 BC, and Pharaoh Shoshenk I circa 925 BC, meaning the town was there for over 500 years. It was the hometown of King David's last concubine, the 12 year old Abishag, who Adonijah attempted to marry after David's death. Some scholars believe that Abishag was the Shulamite this text refers to, or possibly the author of the Song. If this was the work of Abishag, it means that it would date to the time of Solomon, and imply she was one of Solomon's wives or concubines.

2 Codex Vaticanus: Carmêlos (ΚΑΡΜΗΛΟϹ)

• Aleppo Codex: krml (כרמל)

- Leningrad Codex: karmel (כַּרְמֶל֩)
- Targum to Song of Songs: karmelā (כַּרְמְלָא)

Mount Carmel is a prominent mountain in northern modern Israel, near the city of Haifa.

Song of Songs: Chapter 8

I wish that you, my beloved, were he that suckled the breasts of my mother. When I found you, I would kiss you, yes, and they should not hate me. I would take you, I would bring you into my mother's house, and into the room of her, that conceived me. I would make you drink spiced wine and the juice of my pomegranates. His left hand should be under my head, and his right hand should embrace me. I have cursed you, you daughters of Jerusalem, by Sabaoth and the powerful demons, that you don't arouse or awake my love, until he pleases. Who is this that comes up all in white, leaning on her beloved? I raised you up under an apple tree, there your mother brought you out, and there she that carried you brought you out.

Set me as a seal on your heart, like a seal on your arm, for love is strong as death, and jealousy is cruel as the grave. Her shafts are shafts like fire, even wire the flames. A great deal of water will not be able to quench love, and rivers will not drown it. If a man would give all his substance for love, men would completely hate it. Our sister is little, and has no breasts, and what will we do for our sister in the day in which she will be spoken for? If she is a wall, let us build on her silver bulwarks, and if she is a door, let us carve for her cedar panels. I am a wall, and my breasts are as towers, and I was in their eyes like one that found peace. Solomon had a vineyard in Ba'al Hamon, and he rented his vineyard to keepers. Everyone was to bring for its fruit a thousand pieces of silver. My vineyard, even mine, is before me, and Solomon will have a thousand, and they that keep its fruit two hundred. You that live in the gardens, the companions, listen to your voice. Let me hear it. Away, my beloved, and be like a doe or a fawn on the mountains of spices.

Song of Songs: Chapter 8 Notes

1 Codex Vaticanus: Beelamôn (ΒΕΕλΑΜΩΝ)

- Aleppo Codex: bôl hmůn (בעל המון)
- Leningrad Codex: va'al hamon (בַּעַל הָמֹון)
- Targum to Song of Songs: no parallel verse

Wisdom of Solomon: Chapter 1

Love Sydyk,[1] you who are the judges of the Earth.

Think of the Lord[2] with a good heart, and search for him with an innocent heart. He will be found by those who don't tempt him, and he reveals himself to those who don't distrust him. Perverse thoughts separate from God,[3] and his power, when it is tested, and convict the foolish.

Sophia[4] will not enter into a malicious mind,[5] nor live in the body that is subject to sin, as the sacred spirit of discipline will flee from deceit, and leave thoughts that are without understanding and will not stay when unrighteousness comes in. Sophia is a loving spirit, and will not acquit a blasphemer from his words, as God is a witness of his reins and a true witness of his heart, and hears his words.

The spirit of the Lord fills the inhabited world,[6] and that which contains all things knows the voice. Therefore, he who speaks unrighteous things can't hide, and vengeance will not pass by him when it punishes him. Inquisition will be made into the counsels of the ungodly, and the sound of his words will come to the Lord for the manifestation of his wicked deeds. The ear of jealousy hears all things, and the noise of murmurings is not hidden. Therefore, beware of murmuring, which is unprofitable, and hold back your tongue from backbiting, for there are no words so secret that count as nothing, and the mouth that lies kills the mind.

Don't seek death through the errors of your life, and don't pull destruction on yourselves with the works of your hands.

God did not make Mot,[7] and he does not take pleasure in the destruction of the living. He created all things that they might live, and the generations of the cosmos were healthy, and there was no poison of destruction in them, nor Kingdom of Sheol in Adamma.[8]

The righteous are immortal.

The ungodly men, along with their works and words, called it to them when they thought to have it as their friend, and they are consumed to nothing and made a covenant with it because they are worthy to take part in it.

Wisdom of Solomon: Chapter 1 Notes

1 Codex Vaticanus: dicaeosynên (ⲇⲓⲕⲁⲓⲟⲥⲨⲚⲎⲚ).
Translation: righteousness (or justice)

In sections of the Septuagint that were also translated into Hebrew, dicaeosynên (δικαιοσύνην) and dicaeosynês (δικαιοσύνησ) were the translation used where the Masoretic texts retain tzedek (צֶדֶק). In addition to being the Canaanite word for "justice," sdq was also the name of the Canaanite god of justice, recorded in the Bronze Age as Ṣdq (𐎕𐎄𐎖) in Ugaritic, and in the Iron Age as Ṣdq (𐤑𐤃𐤒) in Phoenician. During the Classical Era, the Greeks translated the name as Sydyk (Συδυκ), and during the Roman occupation of Judea, the name Tzedek (צֶדֶק) was the Hebrew translation of the Roman god "Jupiter" (Jovis), and as such continues to be the Hebrew name of the planet Jupiter. In his 4th century AD work Praeparatio Evangelica, the Christian historian Eusebius of Caesarea quoted Philo of Byblos' 2nd century AD translation of Sanchuniathon's Bronze Age Phoenician History, which reported that Misor and Sydyk were the Canaanite gods of equality and justice.

2 Codex Vaticanus: cyriou (ΚΥΡΙΟΥ). Translation: lord (or master, owner)

Assuming the records of the translation of the Septuagint are correct, then the Wisdom of Solomon was translated from an Aramaic text, which would have read either ådny (𐡀𐡃𐡍𐡉) or bôlå (𐡁𐡏𐡋𐡀) where the Greek translation has cyriou (κυρίου). Both terms translate as "lord," "owner," or "master."

3 Codex Vaticanus: theou (ΘΕΟΥ). Translation: god

If the Wisdom of Solomon was translated from an Aramaic source, the word translated as God (θεοῦ) would have been ålh (𐡀𐡋𐡄), the Aramaic word meaning god, and the Aramaic translation of El, recorded as An (𒀭) in Akkadian Cuneiform, îl (𐎛𐎍) in Ugaritic, ål (𐤀𐤋) in Phoenician, ål (ࠀࠋ) in Samaritan, and el (אֵל) in Hebrew, the name of the highest God of the Canaanite pantheon.

4 Codex Vaticanus: Sophia (ϹΟΦΙΑ) Translation: Sophia (or wisdom)

The spirit Sophia is mentioned extensively in the books related to Solomon, and is normally translated into English as the 'spirit of Wisdom.' The equivalent term used in the Masoretic texts is chachamot (חֲכָמוֹת), a feminine plural indefinite form of chacham (חָכָם), meaning "wise" or "smart." The Aramaic word hkm (חֲכַל) likewise meant "to be wise," however, the plural infinite implies the concept of wisdom, and the feminine form implies a goddess of wisdom. The Septuagint's Sophia appears to have been the basis of the Gnostic aeon (or angel) Sophia, as this "Wisdom" is described being sentient. As the term used here denotes a sentient spirit, the Greek Sophia is used in the translation, as there are no records of a Canaanite or Aramean goddess named Hakamot.

5 Codex Vaticanus: psychê (ΨΥΧΗ). Translation: mind (or personality, psyche)

Masoretic equivalent in other books is npš (נֶפֶשׁ) which translates as mind, life, soul, person.

6 Codex Vaticanus: oecoumenên (ΟΙΚΟΥΜΕΝΗΝ). Translation: inhabited world

7 Codex Vaticanus: thanaton (ΘΑΝΑΤΟΝ). Translation: Thanatos (or death, corpse)

Thanatos was the Greek god of death, whose name was used as a translation of Mot from the Masoretic texts. Mot was the

Canaanite god of death, who fought Ba'al in the Ugaritic texts
from the late Bronze Age. The Canaanite name is restored in
this translation.

8 Codex Vaticanus: adou basilion epi gês (ΑΔΟΥΒΑCΙΛΕΙΟΝ
ΕΠΙΓΗC). Translation: Hades' kingdom in (or on, with, near)
Ge (or land, Earth)

Hades was used a a translation in the Septuagint for the
name Sheol found in the Masoretic texts, while Ge was used
as a translation for both the names Eretz and Adama found in
the Masoretic texts. This makes it unclear which goddess was
originally being referenced, however, Adama was the
goddess of the underworld in Canaanite mythology, while
Eretz was the goddess of the surface, suggesting the original
goddess was Adama. Both Canaanite names are restored in
this translation.

Wisdom of Solomon: Chapter 2

The ungodly said, thinking to themselves, but not correctly, "Our life is short and tedious, and in the death of a man there is no remedy, and no known man has returned from the grave. We are born to any hazard, and we will be after this, as if we had never been, for the breath in our nostrils is like smoke, and a little spark in the beating of our heart will be extinguished. Our bodies will be turned to ashes, and our spirits will vanish like the soft air. Our name will be forgotten in time, and no man will remember our works and our life will pass away like the trace of a cloud and will be dispersed like a mist that is driven away by the rays of the sun and consumed with its heat. Our time is a very shadow that passes away, and after our end, there is no return. It is sealed tightly so that no man comes back. Therefore, come on and let's enjoy the good things that are around, and let's quickly use the creatures like in youth. Let's fill ourselves with expensive wine and ointments, and let no flower of the spring pass by us."

"Let's crown ourselves with rosebuds before they are withered. Let none of us go without his part of our voluptuousness. Let's leave tokens of our joyfulness everywhere, for this is our portion, and this is our lot. Let's oppress the poor righteous man, and let's not spare the widow, or revere the ancient gray hairs of the aged. Let our strength be the law of Sydyk, for that which is weak is found to be worth nothing. Therefore let's lie in wait for the righteous, because he is not for our kind, and he is clean, contrary to our ways. He finds fault with our offending the law, and objects to our infamy and the transgressing of our education. He professes to have knowledge of God, and he calls himself the servant of the Lord. He was made to censure our thoughts. He is terrible to us even to see, for his life is not like other men's, his ways are of another kind."

"We are viewed by him as frauds. He avoids our ways like he avoids uncleanliness. He pronounces the end of the just to be blessed and falsely claims that God is his father. Let's see if his words are true, and let's prove what will happen at the end of him. For if the just man is the son of God, he will help him and deliver him from the hand of his enemies. Let's examine him with hatred and torture, so that we may know his meekness, and prove his patience. Let's condemn him with a shameful death, for by his own words he will be respected."

Such things they imagined and were deceived, for their own wickedness has blinded them. As for the mysteries of God, they didn't know them. Neither did they hope for the wages of righteousness, or discerne a reward for guiltless minds. God created man to be immortal and made him an image of his own immortality. Jealously the slanderer Mot[1] came into the cosmos. Tested by him, they find their inheritance real.

Wisdom of Solomon: Chapter 2 Notes

1 Codex Vaticanus: phthonô de diabolou Thanatos (ⲫⲐⲞⲚⲰⲒ ⲆⲈ ⲆⲒⲀⲂⲞⲗⲞⲨ ⲐⲀⲚⲀⲦⲞⲤ). Translation: jealously the slander (or devil) Thanatos (or death)

In the Greek translation of Job, the term diabolô (διαβόλω), meaning "slanderer," was used in places where the Masoretic texts use the term Satan (שָׂטָן), meaning "adversary." The term diabolô (διαβόλω) subsequently came to mean "devil" in Greek and several Greek-influenced languages, while Satan came to viewed as the devil's name in most Christian denominations.

The Greek term Thanatos (Θάνατος) is both the proper name of the god of death, and the word meaning "death" (θάνατος). The name Thanatos was used in the Septuagint where the Masoretic texts use the name Mavet (מָוֶת) or Mût (מות), which was interpreted as the messenger of death within the Second Temple Era Judaism. As a result, Thanatos was interpreted as the angel of death in early Christianity. Mût was also the name of the Canaanite god of death, recorded as Mt (𐎎𐎚) in Ugaritic during the Bronze Age, Mt (𐤌𐤕) in Phoenician, and Mûtå (מותא) in Aramaic. As the Aramaic texts the Greeks translated could not have been about Thanatos, the Semitic name Mot is used in this translation.

Wisdom of Solomon: Chapter 3

The minds of the righteous are in the hands of God, and no torment will touch them. In the sight of the unwise, they seem to die, and their departure is considered miserable. Their leaving us is seen as complete destruction, but they are at peace. Though they are punished in the sight of men, their hope is for immortality. Having been a little chastised, they will be greatly rewarded, for God tested them, and found them worthy for himself. Like gold in the furnace, he tested them and received them like a burnt offering.

In the time of their visitation, they will shine, and run to and fro like sparks among the stubble. They will judge the nations, and have dominion over the people, and their Lord will reign forever. They that put their trust in him will understand the truth, and be faithful in love, and will live with him, for grace and mercy are for his saints, and he cares for his chosen.

The ungodly will be punished according to their own imaginations, which have neglected the righteous, and forgotten the Lord. Whoever despises wisdom and nurture, is miserable, and their hope is vain, their labors unfruitful, and their works unprofitable. Their wives are foolish, and their children wicked. Their descendants are cursed.

Therefore, blessed is the barren that is a virgin, who has not known the sinful bed. She will have fruit in the visitation of minds. Blessed is the eunuch, which with his hands has worked no iniquity, or imagined wicked things against God, as the special gift of faith will be given to him, and an inheritance in the temple of the Lord more acceptable to his mind. Glorious is the fruit of good labor, and the root of wisdom will never fall away. As for the children of adulterers, they will not come to their perfection, and the seed of an unrighteous bed will be searched for. For though they live long, they will still be regarded as nothing, and their old age will be without honor. Or, if they die quickly, they have no hope or comfort on the day of trial. Horrible is the end of the unrighteous generation.

Wisdom of Solomon: Chapter 4

It is better to have no children and to be virtuous, which is remembered forever because it is known by God and men. When it is present, men take it as an example, and when it is gone, they desire it. It wears a crown, and triumphs forever, having taken the victory, striving for pure rewards. But the multiplying brood of the ungodly will not thrive, or take deep root from bastard slips, or lay any strong foundation. Though they flourish in branches for a time, they will not last, and they will be shaken with the wind, and through the force of winds, they will be found out.

The imperfect branches will be broken off, their fruit will be unprofitable, not ripe to eat, and good for nothing. Children begotten of unlawful beds are witnesses of wickedness against their parents in their trial. Though the righteous is prevented from death, he is at peace. Honorable age is not that which stands in the length of time or that which is measured by the number of years. Sophia is the gray hair for men, and a spotless life is better than old age. He pleased God and was beloved by him so that living among sinners he was translated. Yes, quickly he was taken away, in case that wickedness should alter his understanding, or deceit deceive his mind.

The bewitching of vanity obscures that which is true, and the wandering of lust undermines the innocent mind. Being made perfect for a short time, lasts a long time. His mind pleased the Lord, who, therefore, quickened him to take him away from among the wicked. The people saw this but didn't understand it, or remember it in their minds, that his grace and mercy are with his saints, and that he respects his chosen. Therefore, the righteous that have died will condemn the ungodly who are living, and youth that is quickly perfected will judge those with many years and old age of the unrighteous.

They will see the end of the wise, and will not understand what God, in his counsel, has decreed of him, and to what end the Lord has set him in safety. They will see him, and despise him, but God will laugh and scorn them, and they will from then forward be a vile carcass, and a reproach among the dead forever. For he will rend them, and throw them down head first, and they will be speechless. He will shake them from the foundation, and they will be completely laid waste, and be in sorrow, and their memory will die. When they review the records of their sins, they will come with fear, and their own iniquities will convince them to their face.

Wisdom of Solomon: Chapter 5

The righteous man will stand boldly before the faces of those who have afflicted him and made no account of his labors. When they see it, they will be troubled by terrible fear and will be amazed at the strangeness of his salvation, so far beyond what they looked for. Their repenting and groaning for anguish of spirit will think to themselves, "This was he, who we had sometimes insulted, and used as a proverb of reproach. We foolishly thought his life madness, and his end to be without honor. How is he counted among the children of God, and his lot among the saints? We have erred from the way of truth, and the light of righteousness has not shined for us, and the sun of righteousness did not rise above us. We tiered ourselves out in the way of wickedness and destruction. Yes, we have gone through deserts, where there way station, but as for the way of the Lord, we have not known it."

"What has pride profited us? What good has our boasting of riches brought us? All those things have passed away like a shadow, and like a post that rushed by, like a ship that passes over the waves of the water, which when it is gone by, the trace it can't be found, neither the pathway of the keel in the waves. Like a bird that has flown through the air, there is no pathway of hers to be found, but only the sound of her light wings beating the air as she passed through, and afterward, there is no sign of where she went. Or, like when an arrow is shot at a target, it parts the air, which immediately comes together again, so that a man can't know where it went through. We are like this, as soon as we were born, we began to approach our end, and had no sign of virtue to show, but were consumed in our own wickedness."

The hope of the ungodly is like dust that is blown away with the wind, like a thin froth that is driven away with the storm, like the smoke that is dispersed here and there with a tempest and passes away like the memory of a guest that stays only a day. But the righteous live forever, their reward is also with the Lord and the Highest cares for them. Therefore, they will receive a glorious kingdom, and a beautiful crown from the Lord's hand, for, with his right hand will he cover them, and with his arm will he protect them. He will zealously armor and arm the creatures for the revenge of his enemies. He will put on the breastplate of justice, and true judgment as a helmet. He will take equity as an invincible shield. His severe anger will sharpen for a sword, and the cosmos will fight alongside him against the unwise.

Then thunderbolts will descend from the clouds like water from a well, as from the drawn bow, will they fly to the target. Hailstones full of anger will be hurled as if from a sling, and the water of the sea will rage against them and cruelly flood them. A mighty wind will stand up against them, and like a tornado will blow them away. Their iniquity will reduce the whole earth to a desert, and wickedness will overthrow the thrones of the mighty.

Wisdom of Solomon: Chapter 6

Sophia is better than strength, and a wise man is better than a strong man. Therefore, listen you kings, and understand. Learn, you who are judges of the ends of the earth. Listen, you who rule the people, and revel in the multitude of nations.

Power is given to you by the Lord, and sovereignty from the Highest,[1] who will examine your works, and search your thoughts. If being administrators of his kingdom, you have not judged correctly, or kept the law, or followed the counsel of God, then quickly and terribly he will come against you, and a sharp judgment will be for those who are in high places. Mercy will quickly pardon the lowly, but mighty men will be tortured greatly. He who is Lord over all will fear no man, neither will he stand in awe of any man's greatness, for he has made the small and great, and cares for all equally, and a terrible trial will come from the mighty.

Therefore, I speak to you kings, that you may learn wisdom, and not be lost. Those who keep the justice just will be judged justified, and those who have learned these things will learn how to decide. Therefore, set your affection on my words and desire them, and you will be instructed. Sophia is glorious and never fades away. She is easily seen by those who love her and found by those who seek her. She prevents those that desire her, from finding her at first. Whoever seeks her early will have no great journey, for he will find her sitting at his doors. Therefore, to think about her is the perfection of wisdom, and whoever looks for her will quickly be without care, for she goes about seeking those that are worthy of her, showing herself favorably to them in many ways, and meeting them in every thought. Her principle is the desire for true education, and careful education is her love. Love is following her Torah, and paying attention to her Torah is the assurance of purity. Purity makes us near to God, therefore the desire of Sophia brings one to the kingdom. If your delight is then in thrones and scepters, you kings of the people, honor Sophia, that you may reign forever.

As for Sophia, what she is, and how she arose, I will tell you, and will not hide the mysteries from you, but will search her out from the beginning of her birth, and bring the knowledge of her into the light, and will not omit the truth. Neither will I go with consuming envy, for such a man will have no fellowship with Sophia. The multitude of the wise is the welfare of the cosmos, and a wise king will raise his people. Therefore, receive instruction through my words, and it will do you good.

Wisdom of Solomon: Chapter 6 Notes

1 Codex Vaticanus: ypsistou (ΥϯΙⲤΤΟΥ). Translation: highest

• Septuagint manuscript 261: ypsistô (υΨιστω). Translation: loftiest

This term was also used in Cosmic Genesis, where the Hebrew parallel in Bereshít is ôlyŭn (עֶלְיוֹן), which translates as "highest." The "highest god" was also listed as a god in the Sefire Treaty from circa 750 BC as ål ůålyn (𐤉‌𐤋‌𐤀‌‌ 𐤋‌𐤀), meaning "God and Highest" in Aramaic. The Greek translations of Sanchuniathon's Bronze Age writing that have survived to the present, referred to the primordial creator god of the Canaanites as Elioun (Ελιουν), which appears to be the same god. According to Sanchuniathon, Elioun was the "highest" (υψιστος) god, who made the sky and the land, and they made the rest of the gods.

Wisdom of Solomon: Chapter 7

I myself also am a mortal man, like all, and the offspring of he who was first made on the earth. In my mother's womb, I was fashioned to be flesh over the course of ten months, being formed in blood, from the seed of man, and the pleasure that came with sleep.

When I was born, I breathed the common air and fell to the ground, which is of similar nature The first voice which I uttered was crying, as all others do. I was nursed in swaddling clothes with great care. There is no king that had any other beginning except birth, for all men have one entrance into life, and the same leaving it. Therefore I prayed, and understanding was given to me. I called on God, and the spirit Sophia came to me. I preferred her to scepters and thrones and saw riches as nothing in comparison to her. I did not compare her to any precious stone, because all gold in comparison to her is like a little sand, and silver will be counted as clay before her. I loved her above health and beauty, and chose to have her instead of light, for the light that comes from her never goes out.

All good things came to me through her, and innumerable riches from her hands. I rejoiced in them all because wisdom comes before them, and I did not know that she was the mother of them. I learned diligently and communicated with her liberally. I did not hide her riches, for she is a treasure-house to men that never fails, through which they use it to become friends with God, being commended for the gifts that come from learning.

God has allowed me to speak as I would, and to conceive my thoughts worthy of those who are given me, because it is he who leads to Sophia, and directs the wise. In his hand, are both we and our words, also all wisdom, and skill of workmanship. He has given me certain knowledge of the things that are, namely, how the cosmos was made, the operation of the elements, the beginning, ending, and in-between times, and the patterns of the movements of the Sun, the change of seasons, the circuits of years, and the positions of stars, the natures of living creatures, and the furies of wild beasts, the forces of winds, and the reasoning of men, the diversities of plants and the virtues of roots, all similar things that are either secret or known, them I know.

Sophia works through all things and has taught me. In her is the spirit that is intelligent, sacred, subtle in many ways, eloquent, active, pure, sure, sweet, loving that which is good, quick, which nothing can slow down, beneficent, kind, steadfast, assuring, carefree, all-powerful, all-seeing, intelligible, and encompassing all spirits. Sophia is faster than any moving thing, and she passes and goes through all things because of her pureness. She is the breath of the god Sabaoth,[1] and a pure influence flowing from the glory of the Almighty, therefore no defiled thing can fall into her. For she is the brightness of the everlasting light, the spotless mirror of the power of God, and the image of his goodness. Being only one, she can still do all things, and remaining in herself she renews all things, and in all ages enters into pure minds, she makes them friends of God, and prophets. God loves none but him that lives with wisdom, for she is more beautiful than Shemesh,[2] and above all the star constellations.[3] Compared to the light, she comes first, for after this comes night, but vice will not prevail against Sophia.

Wisdom of Solomon: Chapter 7 Notes

1 Codex Vaticanus: theou dynameôs (ΘΕΟΥΔΥΝΑΜΕѠϹ). Translation: god forces

This appears to have been a reference to the "god Sabaoth" in the Aramaic text, which was translated literally. This suggests the book was translated later than most of the Israelite texts, as this god was known as Sabaoth (Σαβαωθ) by Hellenistic Judeans, Dionysus (Διονύσιος) by Greeks, and Sabazios (Σαβάζιος) by the Phrygians. The syncretic god was invented by the last Egyptian Pharaoh Nectanebo II in 344 BC as a common war god for his armies and Greek, Macedonian, Phygian, Judean, Carthaginian, and Roman mercenaries. He initiated the cult of Buchis (Ⲃⲩⲱϩ), in which a bull was slaughtered each year, that was believed to be the incarnation of the Egyptian war god Montu. The name drew from the older Bacchae (Βάκχαι) play that was done each year during the City Dionysia festival in Greece and Macedonia.

This cult was imported into the Roman Republic as the cult of Bacchus, primarily from the Greek worship of Dionysus, which involved wine and orgies. During the Second Punic War (218-201 BC), the Romans nationalized the cult of Bacchus to remove the Carthaginian influence and united it with the older cult of Liber, the old Latin god of wine. The Phrygian and Judean versions of the god were closer to the Egyptian war god, as Sabaoth (Σαβαωθ) was interpreted in Hebrew as ṣbảůt (צְבָאוֹת), meaning "armies," and Sabazios (Σαβάζιος) was the supreme God, who rode into war on a flying horse. The Aramaic interpretation of the word ṣbảůt (צבאות) was closer to the Greek, as it meant "desires."

The Maccabean revolt, as described in the various Maccabean literature, appears to have been largely caused by the Phrygian priest Philip becoming the high priest at the temple in Jerusalem. During the initial revolt, the issue appears to have been that the god Sabaoth was being equated with foreign gods. The Septuagint's 2nd Maccabees, which claims to be an abridged version of Jason of Cyrene's now lost five-volume version of Maccabees, referred to the false god being worshipped in the temple as Dionysus. The Septuagint's 1st Maccabees, which was written later, referred to the god Sabaoth as the god of Jason, the leader of the revolt, which the medieval Hebrew Maccabees confirms. Sabaoth does not appear to have been suppressed until after the

Hasmonean dynasty was established when the term ṣbâût (צבאות) was demoted to an epithet of the god Yhůh (יהוה).

2 Codex Vaticanus: Êliou (ΗΛΙΟΥ). Translation: Helios (or sun)

The Masoretic equivalent in other books is Shemesh (שֶׁמֶשׁ), which was both the word for "sun" and the name of the sun god. His worship was banned in Judah by King Josiah circa 625 BC.

3 Codex Vaticanus: astrôn thesin (ΑCΤΡωΝ ΘΕCΙΝ). Translation: stars (or fates) settings (or placements, arrangements)

• Septuagint manuscript 766: aesthêsin (ΔΙϹΘΛϹΙΝ).

Translation: senses (or perceptions)

The Greek translation does not use the translation for "constellations," asterismos (ἀαστερισμός), meaning "star markings," nevertheless the Greek translation does appear to be very similar to the Hebrew term kevutzat kochavim (קְבוּצַת כּוֹכָבִים), meaning "group of stars." A similar term was used in Aramaic, qybůṣ kůkbyn (ןיבכוכ תצובק), meaning "community of stars," which the Greek translators appear to have translated as astrôn thesin (ἀστρων θέσιν). This supports the book having been translated from Aramaic.

Wisdom of Solomon: Chapter 8

The might of Sophia reaches from one end to the other, and she sweetly orders all things.

I loved her, and searched for her from my youth, desired to make her my bride, and became a lover of her beauty. She magnifies her nobility by conversing with God, and the Lord of all things himself loved her. She teaches the mysteries of the knowledge of God and is a lover of his works. If riches are a possession to be desired in this life, what is richer than the wisdom that makes all things?

If the desire to create, who of all that exists is a more creative worker than she? If a man loves righteousness, her works are virtues, as she teaches temperance and prudence, justice, and fortitude. Men can have nothing more profitable in their lives. If a man desires great knowledge, she knows the history and correctly predicts what is to come. She knows the subtleties of speech and can settle arguments. She foresees signs and wonders, and the events of seasons and times. Therefore I decided to take her to me to live with me, knowing that she would be a good counselor, and would comfort me in my care and grief.

For her sake, I am highly esteemed by many, and honored by the elders, though I am young. I will be found to be quick in judgment and will be admired in the sight of great men. When I hold my tongue, they will wait, and when I speak, they will listen to me. If I talk much, they will keep their mouths closed. Through her, I will achieve immortality, and leave behind me an everlasting memory to those who come after me. I will organize the people, and nations will be subject to me. Horrible tyrants will be afraid when they only hear about me. I will be judged good by the multitude, and be valiant in war. After I have come into my house, I will rest with her, as there is no bitterness in her conversation, and living with her has no sorrow, but humor and joy.

Now, when I considered these things myself and pondered them in my heart, how that being allied to Sophia is immortality, the great pleasure it is to have her friendship, that in the works of her hands are infinite riches, and through her council comes wisdom, and through talking with her comes glory, I traveled around searching for how to take her to me.

I was a witty child and had a good spirit. Being good, I grew into a pure body. Nevertheless, when I learned that I could not otherwise obtain her, except if God gave her to me, and that was a point of Sophia, to know whose gift she was, I prayed to the Lord and begged him with my whole heart. I said, [Continued in the next chapter.]

Wisdom of Solomon: Chapter 9

[Continued from the previous chapter,] "God of my forefathers, and Lord of mercy, who has made all things through your words, who has appointed man through your wisdom, that he should have dominion over the creatures which you have made, so he could order the cosmos according to Misor and Sydyk,[1] and execute judgment with an upright heart. Give me Sophia, who sits by your throne, and don't reject me from among your children, for I, your servant, and son of your handmaid am a feeble man, of a short time, and am too young to understand judgment and laws."

"Even if a man is perfect among the children of men, yet your wisdom is not within him, he will be regarded as nothing. You have chosen me to be king of your people, and judge of your sons and daughters. You have commanded me to build a temple on your holy mount, and an altar in the city in which you live resembling the holy tabernacle, which you prepared in the beginning. Sophia was with you. She knows your works and was present when you made the cosmos and knew what was acceptable in your sight, and right in your commandments. Send her down out of your pure sky, and from your majestic throne, so she may work with me, and that I may know what is acceptable to you."

"She knows and understands all things, and she will lead me soberly in my works, and preserve me through her power. Then my works will be acceptable, and then will I judge your people justly, and be worthy to sit in my father's throne. What man can know the counsel of God? Who can fathom the will of the Lord? The thoughts of mortal men are miserable, and our counselors are uncertain. The corruptible body holds down the mind, and the earthy home weighs down the minds that muse on many things. With difficulty we guess correctly at things that are on earth, and with work do we find the things that are right before us, but the things that are in the sky who has understood? Who has known your counsel, except those you give Sophia? So send your sacred spirit from above! The ways of those who lived on the Earth were reformed, and men were taught the things that are pleasing to you, and were saved through Sophia."

Wisdom of Solomon: Chapter 9 Notes

1 Codex Vaticanus: osiotêti cae dicaeosynê (ⲞⲤⲒⲞⲦⲎⲦⲒⲔⲀⲒ ⲆⲒⲔⲀⲒⲞⲤⲨⲚⲎ). Translation: righteousness and justice

In sections of the Septuagint that were also translated into Hebrew, dicaeosynên (δικαιοσύνην) and dicaeosynê (δικαιοσύνη) were the translation used where the Aleppo Codex retains sdq (צדק). In addition to being the Canaanite word for "justice," sdq was also the name of the Canaanite god of justice, recorded in the Bronze Age as Ṣdq (𒁹𒅎—◀) in Ugaritic, and in the Iron Age as Ṣdq (𐤑𐤃𐤒) in Phoenician. During the Classical Era, the Greeks translated the name as Sydyk (Συδυκ), and during the Roman occupation of Judea, the name Ṣedeq (צֶדֶק) was the Hebrew translation of the Roman god "Jupiter," and as such continues to be the Hebrew name of the planet Jupiter. In his 4th century AD work Praeparatio Evangelica, the Christian historian Eusebius of Caesarea quoted Philo of Byblos' 2nd century AD translation of Sanchuniathon's Bronze Age Phoenician History, which reported that Misor and Sydyk were the Canaanite gods of fairness and justice.

In addition to being the Canaanite word for "fairness," Misor (𐤌𐤉𐤔𐤓) was also the name of the Canaanite god of fairness, and appears to be what the Greeks translated as hosiotêti (ὁσιότητι), a word meaning "observing divine law" and loosely translated as "righteousness." Unlike Sydyk, the name Misor does not appear not have been translated consistently in the Septuagint, likely because the god was no longer being worshiped when the Greek translation was made. The name was also transliterated as Misôr (Μισωρ) in some places, notably in Joshua, where it was the name of a village named after the god.

Misor and Sydyk were treated as a pair of gods throughout early Semitic history. The earliest surviving mention of the pair of gods is believed to be Mešar and Išar recorded in the Mari Cuneiform tablets from the 3rd millennium BC. The Mari Cuneiform tablets are from the ancient city of Mari, on the Euphrates River in eastern modern Syria. The tablets are written in a different language from the Akkadian Cuneiform tablets found in the territory of modern Iraq, however, used the same symbols. Depending on the translator, they are interpreted as an early form of the Canaanite language, a precursor to the Aramaic language, or another Semitic language separate from both the Western and Eastern Semitic language branches. However the language is interpreted, the gods Mešar and Išar as accepted as early versions of Misor and Sydyk, which then also means the Akkadian equivalents of Mešar and Išar, recorded as Misharu and Kittu, are the Akkadian equivalents of Misor and Sydyk.

Wisdom of Solomon: Chapter 10

[Continued from the previous chapter,] "She preserved the first-formed father of the cosmos, who was created alone, and brought him out of his fall, and gave him the power to rule all things."

"When the unrighteous left her in his anger, he also perished in the fury when he murdered his brother, for whose cause the earth was drowned with the flood. Sophia again preserved it, and directed the course of the righteous in a piece of wood of small value."

"Moreover, when the nations in their wicked conspiracy were confused, she searched for the righteous, and preserved he who was blameless to God, and kept him strong against his tender compassion towards his son."

"When the ungodly perished, she delivered the righteous man, who fled from the fire which fell down on the five cities, of whose wickedness the wasteland that smokes is a testimony even to this day, where plants bear fruit that never ripens, and a standing pillar of salt is a monument of an unbelieving mind. In disregarding Sophia, they not only received this punishment, but those who were ignorant of good things also left behind a memorial of their foolishness to the cosmos, so that in the things in which they offended would not be forgotten."

"However, Sophia has delivered from pain those that attended to her. When the righteous fled from his brother's anger she guided him through right paths, showed him the kingdom of God, and gave him knowledge of holy things, made him rich in his travels, and multiplied the fruit of his labors."

"During the deceit of those that oppressed him, she stood by him and made him rich. She defended him from his enemies and kept him safe from those that lay in wait, and in a terrible battle she gave him victory, that he might know that goodness is stronger than all."

"When the righteous was sold, she did not forget him but delivered him from sin. She went down with him into the pit and did not leave him in shackles until she brought him the scepter of the kingdom and power over those who oppressed him. As for those that had accused him, she showed them to be liars, and gave him perpetual glory."

"She delivered the righteous people and blameless seed from the nation that oppressed them. She entered into the mind of the servant of the Lord and withstood dreadful kings through wonders and signs, rendered to the righteous a reward of their labors, marvelously guiding them, and was for them for a cover by day, and a light from the stars in the nighttime. She brought them through the Papyrus Sea[1] and led them through great waters, yet she drowned their enemies, and through them up out of the bottom of the deep. Therefore the just took the spoils of the wicked, and praised your holy name, Lord, and magnified your hand that fought for them with one voice. Sophia opened the mouth of the dumb, and made the tongues eloquent of those that can't speak."

Wisdom of Solomon: Chapter 10 Notes

1 Codex Vaticanus: thalassan erythran (ⲐⲀⲖⲀⲤⲤⲀⲚ ⲈⲢⲨⲐⲢⲀⲚ). Translation: Erythraean Sea

The Greek name translates as the "sea red," which was adopted from the Aramaic ymå hådm (ﬤﬡﬡﬠ ﬡﬤﬠ), meaning "sea of the red." The Aramaic name was adopted from the older Canaanite name ym ådm (ﬤﬠﬡ ﬠﬤ), and Egyptian yům idůmô (𓇌𓂝𓅓 𓇌𓂧𓅓𓈗), both meaning "Sea of Edom." The Edomites were originally recorded as living at the northern end of the Gulf of Aqaba.

The events in the Book of Names (Masoretic Exodus) place the events in the verse at yam-suf (יַם־ס֑וּף), which translates as "sea of papyrus" or "sea of reeds." The name was transliterated directly once in the Codex Vaticanus' book of Judges, as thalassês Siph (θαλάσσησ Σιφ), however, it was generally translated as thalassan Erythran (θαλασσαν Ερυθραν).

The Aramaic word sůf (𐡎𐡅𐡐) and Phoenician word sůf (𐤎𐤅𐤐), both meaning "papyrus plants" were adopted from the Egyptian term tjůfī (𓍿𓅱𓆑𓇅𓏥), which referred to "papyrus," "papyrus plants," and "papyrus marshes." The Egyptian term continued to be used into the Classical era as the Coptic words čoouf (ϫⲟⲟⲩϥ), conf (ϭⲟⲛϥ), and comf (ϭⲟⲙϥ), all meaning papyrus. Conversely, the Egyptian name of the Red Sea was the Sea of Ḥeḥ (𓁨), meaning 'very large sea' from the Middle Kingdom era onward, however, it is believed to have originally been named after the ancient Egyptian frog god Heh (𓎛𓎛𓅱). As the Greek translation of "Erythrean Sea" is anachronistic, the translation of "Papyrus Sea" is imported from the Masoretic text.

Wisdom of Solomon: Chapter 11

[Continued from the previous chapter,] "She blessed their works through the hands of the holy prophet. They traveled through the uninhabited wilderness and pitched tents in places where there was no way station. They stood against their enemies and were avenged by their adversaries. When they were thirsty, they called on you, and water was given them out of the flinty rock, and their thirst was quenched out of the hard stone. Their enemies were punished when their drink failed them, the same way their needs were met, for instead of a fountain of a perpetual running river, you gave the unjust blood."

"A manifest proof of that commandment when the infants were slain, you gave to them an abundance of water by which they had not hoped for, showing through that thirst then how you had killed their adversaries. For when they were tested, and in mercifully chastised, they knew how the ungodly were judged in anger and tortured. These you admonished and tested like a father, but the others you condemned and punished like a terrible tyrant. Whether they were absent or present, they were all tortured, as a double grief came on them, and a groaning for the memory of the past. When they heard by their own punishments the other was to be benefited, they remembered the Lord. He who they had treated with scorn when he was exposed to die, they admired in the end when they saw what happened."

"The foolish counseled their wickedness, where being deceived, they worshiped serpents void of reason and vile beasts, and you sent a multitude of dumb beasts against them for vengeance. So they might know, that however, if a man sins, by the same, he will also be punished. For your Almighty hand, that made the cosmos of formless matter, was not unable to send among them a multitude of bears, fierce lions, or unknown wild beasts of a new kind and full of rage, fire-breathing, emitting filthy smoke, and shooting terrible sparks out of their eyes. This not only harmed them once but also the terrible sight completely demoralized them. Without these, they might have been killed with one blast, perse-cuted in vengeance, and scattered abroad through the breath of your power, but you have ordered all things in measure and number and weight."

"You can show your great strength at all times when you will, and who can withstand the power of your arm? For the whole cosmos is before you like a little grain on the balance, like a drop of the morning dew that falls down on the Earth. Yet, you have mercy on all, for you can do all things, and close your eyes to the sins of men because they repent. You love all the things that are and hate nothing that you have made, for you would not have made it if you hated it. How could anything have endured, if it had not been your will? Or been preserved, if not called by you? You spare all, for they are yours, Lord, who loves the minds."

Wisdom of Solomon: Chapter 12

[Continued from the previous chapter,] "Your incorruptible spirit is in all things, therefore you chasten them little and little who offend, and warn them reminding them of how they have offended, so when they end wickedness they may believe in you, Lord. For it was your will to destroy through the hands of our fathers both the old inhabitants of your sacred land, whom you hated for doing most terrible acts of witchcraft and wicked sacrifices. Also, those merciless child-killers, cannibals, and blood-drinkers, with their priests out of the middle of your consecration, as well as those parents that killed by their own hands the helpless minds, so the land that you considered most sacred to you, might receive a worthy colony of God's children."

"Nevertheless even those you spared as men, and sent wasps before your army, to destroy them by little and little. Not that you were unable to bring the ungodly under the hand of the righteous in battle, or to destroy them at once with cruel beasts, or with one rough word, but executing your judgments on them by little and little, you gave time to repent, being aware that they were a wicked generation, but that their malice was inbred and their thoughts could not be changed. It was a cursed seed from the beginning, and you weren't afraid that any man pardon them for those things they did and say, "What have you done?" Who will withstand your judgment? Who will accuse you of wrongdoing for the nations that die, which you made? Who will come to stand against you, to be revenged for the unrighteous men?"

"There is no god like you that cares for all, who you might show that your judgment is incorrect. Neither will king or tyrant be able to set his face against you, for any who have, you have punished. As much as you are righteous yourself, you order all things righteously, thinking it is not agreeable with your power to condemn him who has not deserved to be punished. For your power is the beginning of righteousness, and because you are the Lord of all, it makes you gracious to all."

"When men will not believe that you are all-powerful, you show your strength, and among them, that know it, you make their boldness manifest. Yet, you hold back your power, judge with equity, and order us with great favor. You could use power when you want, but through such works you have taught your people that the just man should be merciful, and have made your children be good, and hope that you give forgiveness for sins. If you punished the enemies of your children, and the condemned to death, with such deliberation, giving them time and place, where they might be delivered from their malice, how much consideration did you judge your own sons to whose fathers you have sworn with, and made covenants of good promises?"

"Therefore, when you punish us, you scourge our enemies a thousand times worse, to the intent that, when we judge, we should carefully think of your goodness, and when we ourselves are judged, we should look for mercy. Therefore, while men have lived dissolutely and unjustly, you have tortured them with their own abominations, as they went astray very far in the ways of error, and considered the beasts as gods which even their enemies despised, being deceived, like children of no understanding."

"Therefore to them, like children without the use of reason, you sent a judgment to mock them. Those that would not be reformed by that correction, felt a judgment worthy of God. Seeing the indignity they suffered by those they considered god when they were destroyed the same way, they acknowledged him to be the true God, who they had denied before, and therefore the end of their damnation also came for them."

Wisdom of Solomon: Chapter 13

[Continued from the previous chapter,] "Certainly, all men who are ignorant of God are vain by nature. They could not know him who from the good things are seen, nor by considering the works have they acknowledged the craftsman. Instead, they have considered fire, or wind, the circle of the stars, the great sea, or the lights in the sky, to be the gods which govern the cosmos. Those whose beauty they delighted in and took to be gods, know-how greater is the Lord of them, for the first author of beauty has created them. But if they were astonished at their power and virtue, let them understand through them, how much mightier he is that made them, for by the greatness and beauty of the creature, is the creator of them is seen."

"Yet for this, they are to be blamed less, for they error while seeking God, and desire to find him, for being knowledgeable of his works, they search him diligently, and believe their sight because of the beauty of the things that are seen. How is it that they are not pardoned? If they were able to know so much that they could judge the cosmos, how did they not sooner find the Lord? They are miserable, and their hope is in dead things who they call gods, which are the works of men's hands made from gold and silver, are made to resemble beasts or a stone good for nothing, the work of an ancient hand."

"Now a carpenter that fells timber, after he has chopped down a tree right for the purpose, and taken off all the bark skillfully around, and has worked it diligently, and made a vessel from it fit for the service of man's life. After using the remnants of his work to cook his meat, and has filled himself, taking the remnants which served no use, a crooked piece of wood full of knots, he carves it diligently when he had nothing else to do, and formed it by the skill of his understanding, and fashioned it to the image of a man, or some beast, covering it over with vermilion, and with red-colored paint and covering every spot of it, when he has made a convenient room for it, set it in a wall, and fastened with iron. He provided for it that it might not fall, knowing that it was unable to help itself, for it is an image, and needs to be helped. Then he prays for his goods, for his wife and children, and is not ashamed to speak to that which has no life. He calls on that which is weak for health and prays for life to that which is dead. He humbly implores that which has the least means to help for aid, and he asks from that which can't move its feet for a good journey. For gain, and for the success of his hands, and the ability to do things he asks that which is unable to do anything."

Wisdom of Solomon: Chapter 14

[Continued from the previous chapter,] "Again, one preparing himself to sail, and about to pass through the raging waves, calls on a piece of wood more rotten than the vessel that carries him. For the desire of gain devised this, and the workman built it through his skill.

But your providence, Father, governs it, for you have made a way through the sea, and a safe path through the waves, showing that you can be saved from all danger, yes, even if a man goes to sea without art. Nevertheless, you do not want the works of your wisdom to be idle, and therefore men that commit their lives to a small piece of wood, pass through the rough sea in a weak vessel are saved.

In the old times as well, when the proud giants died, the hope of the cosmos escaped in a weak vessel, and left a seed for all generations and to all ages."

"Blessed is the wood through which justice comes, but that which is made with hands is cursed, and also he that made it. He, because he made it, and it, because, being corruptible, it was called God. As the ungodly and his ungodliness are both equally reproachful to God, and that which is made will be punished together with him that made it. Therefore even against the idols of the Gentiles, there will be a visitation, because the creatures of God have become an abomination and stumbling blocks to the minds of men, and a snare to the feet of the unwise.

The invention of idols was the beginning of spiritual fornication, and the creation of them was the corruption of life. Neither were they from the beginning nor will they be forever. Through the vain pride of men, they entered into the cosmos, and therefore will they come shortly to an end. A father afflicted with untimely mourning made an image of his child that was taken away too soon and honored him as a god, which was then a dead man, and appointed to those that were under him ceremonies and sacrifices. Thus in the course of time, an ungodly custom grown strong was kept as a law, and engraved images were worshiped at the commandments of kings. Men who could not honor in presence, because they lived far away, took a copy of his image, and made an express image of a king who they honored so that by this their forwardness they might flatter him who was absent as if he were present. Also, the singular diligence of the craftsman helped to push forward more superstition on the ignorant, for he, perhaps willing to please the one in authority, used all his skill to make the image in the best way. Then the multitude, allured by the grace of the work, took him now for a god, which a little before was hardly honored."

"This was an occasion to deceive the cosmos, for men, serving either calamity or tyranny, ascribed to stones and wood the incommunicable name. Moreover, this was not enough for them, that they erred in the knowledge of God, but while they lived in the great war of ignorance, they called peace 'plagues.' While they killed their children in sacrifices, used secret ceremonies, or made celebrations from strange rites, they neither kept their lives nor marriages pure any longer, but either one killed another traitorously, or insulted him through adultery, so that without exception what ruled men was blood, murder, theft, pretense, corruption, unfaithfulness, confusion, perjury, the disquieting of good men, forgetfulness of God, defiling of minds, changing of nature, disorders in marriages, adultery, and uncleanness."

"The worshiping of idols not to be named is the beginning, the cause, and the end, of all evil. Either, they are mad when they are merry, or prophesy lies, or live unjustly, or else causally swear themselves. Their trust is in idols, which have no life, and so they swear falsely, yet they expect to not be hurt. For both things will they be justly punished, both because they did not think much of God, listening to idols, and also because they have sworn unjustly in deceit, despising justice. As it is not the power of them by whom they swear, but it is the just vengeance of sinners, that always punishes the offense of the unjust."

Wisdom of Solomon: Chapter 15

[Continued from the previous chapter,] "You, God, are gracious and true, patient, and mercifully organize all things. If we sin, we are yours, knowing your power, but if we don't sin, we know that we are counted as yours. To know you is perfect justice, and to know your power is the root of immortality, for neither did the mischievous inventions of men deceive us, or an image painted with various colors, or the fruitless labor of an engraved figure with diverse colors. The sight of this entices fools to lust after it, and so they desire the lifeless figure of a dead image. The lovers of evil things have nothing better to believe in, both those that make them and those that love and worship them."

"The potter also tempers soft earth and fashions every vessel with much labor for our service. Of the same clay, he makes both the vessels that serve for clean uses and those that are unclean. What is the use of either sort? The potter himself is the judge. Employing his labor vainly, he makes a god of the same clay, even though he was just a little earlier part of earth himself, and after a little while after returns to the same, when his life which was lent him will be demanded back."

His concern is not that he will have more work, or that his life is short, but he competes with the goldsmiths and silversmiths, and endeavors to create works like the bronzesmiths, and counts it to his glory to make vain things. His heart is ashes, his hope is vain and earthly. His life is of less value than clay, as he did not know his creator, and he inspired into him an active mind and breathed in a living spirit. But they counted our life as a pastime, and our time here as a business for profit, as, they say, 'We must be gaining in every way, even through evil means.' This man, that of earthly matter makes brittle vessels and engraved images, knows himself to offend above all others."

"All of your people's enemies, who subjugate them, are most foolish, unhappy, and proud beyond calculating, as they counted all the idols of the heathens to be gods, which don't have eyes to see, noses to breathe, ears to hear, fingers and hands to handle, and as for their feet, they are slow to walk. Men made them, and he that borrowed his own spirit fashioned them, but no man can make a god even equal to himself. Being mortal, he worked a dead thing with wicked hands, and he himself is better than the things which he worships, as he lived once, but they never did."

"Some worshiped those vicious animals, yet they don't even have the ability to reason, and are therefore worse than those who worship them. Not only can no one see any good in these beasts, but they have fled from the praise of God and his blessing."

Wisdom of Solomon: Chapter 16

[Continued from the previous chapter,] "Because of this they punished appropriately, and by a multitude of beasts tortured. Instead of which punishment, when dealing graciously with your own people, you prepared for them, a new flavor of meat, preparing quails for them. As they, desiring food, by means of those things that were shown and sent among them, might hate even that which was necessary to satisfy their needs, and by these, allowing their destitution for a short time, so they might be made enjoy a new taste."

"It was required that inevitable destruction should come on those that were tyrannical, but to these, it should only be shown how their enemies were slaughtered. When the horrible fierceness of beasts came on these, and they died by the bites crooked serpents, your did not last forever. They were troubled for a short time, that they might be corrected, having a sign of salvation to remind them of the commandments of your law. He that turned himself towards it, was not saved by the thing that he saw, but by you, that is the savior of all. In this, you showed your enemies that it is you who delivers from all evil."

"The bites of locusts and flies killed them, and there was no remedy for their life because they were worthy to be punished by such things. Yet, not even the teeth of venomous dragons overcame your children, as your mercy came and healed them. They were tested so that they would remember your words and were quickly saved, to avoid falling into deep forgetfulness, and so they might always remember your goodness. It was neither plant, nor mollifying plaster, that healed them to health, but your word, Lord, which heals all things."

"You have the power of life and death, you lead to the gates of Hades,[1] and bring back again. A man indeed kills through his malice, and the spirit, when it has left does not return, but neither can the mind be called back with has been taken. It is not possible to escape your hands. The wicked who denied you were scourged by the strength of your arm and were persecuted by strange storms, hail, and rain that they could not avoid, and they were consumed by fire. What is more wonderful is that the fire had more force in the water, which extinguished all things, for the cosmos fights for the righteous. For some time the flame was mitigated, that it might not burn up the beasts that were sent against the wicked, that they might see and understand that they were persecuted by the judgment of God. At another time it burned even in the water greater than the power of fire, that it might destroy the fruits of an unjust land."

"Instead you fed your own people with angels' food and sent them from the sky bread prepared without labor, able to satisfy everyone's appetite and agreeing with everyone's taste. Your sustenance declared your sweetness to your children, and serving as the appetite of the eater tempered itself to every man's preference."

"Snow and ice endured the fire and did not melt, that they might see the fire burning in the hail and sparks in the rain destroying the fruits of their enemies. This again was the same way that they just were nourished. For the creatures that serve you their creator, become fierce against the unjust for their punishment and abate his strength for the benefit of those that put their trust in you. Therefore, even then was it altered into all things, and was obedient to your grace, which nourishes all things according to the desire of those who were in need, so your children, Lord, who you love, might know, that it is not the growing of fruits that nourishes man, but that it is your word, which preserves them those put their trust in you. That which was not destroyed by the fire, being warmed with a little sunlight, soon melted away, so we might know, that we must give thanks to you, Shachar,[2] and bow down to the eastern light.[3] For the hope of the ungrateful will melt away like the winter's ice and will run away as unusable water."

Wisdom of Solomon: Chapter 16 Notes

1 Codex Vaticanus: adou (αδου). Translation: Hades

2 Codex Vaticanus: Êlion (ΗΛΙΟΝ). Translation: Helios (or sun)

• Codex Venetus: orthron (ΟΡΘΡΟΝ). Translation: dawn (or morning twilight)

• Septuagint Manuscript 543: êlion phthanin (ἡλιον φθανϭιν). Translation: sun beforehand (or before sun)

The Hebrew equivalent in other books was Shemesh (שֶׁמֶשׁ), which was both the word for sun, and the name of the god of the sun. Shemesh's worship was banned by King Josiah in Judah circa 625 BC. In this verse, the parallel text in the Codex Venetus and LXX 543 indicated the original word was probably šhrå (שׁחרא), meaning "dawn" or "pre-dawn light." As the verse is referring to a god that is prayed to at dawn, this would have been the Canaanite god Šhr (𐤔𐤄𐤓), commonly called Shachar, the Canaanite god of dawn.

3 Codex Vaticanus: anatolên phôtos entynchaninlion (ΑΝΑΤΟΛΗΝ ΦΩΤΟC ΕΝΤΥΓΧΑΝΕΙΝ). Translation: eastern light I bow down (or fall before, entreat)

• Codex Sinaiticus: anatolês tou phôtos entynchanin (ΑΝΑΤΟΛΗC ΤΟΥ ΦΩΤΟC ΕΝΤΥΓΧΑΝΕΙΝ). Translation: east to the light I bow down (or fall before, entreat)

Praying to the east at dawn is one of the things that King Josiah specifically banned circa 625 BC, meaning this book must have been written before that.

Wisdom of Solomon: Chapter 17

[Continued from the previous chapter,] "Great are your judgments, and can't be described, and therefore immature minds have erred. When unjust men wanted to oppress the holy nation, they themselves were shackled in chains of darkness and locked in their houses by the bonds of a long night, lay, therefore, were exiled from the eternal providence. While they thought to lie and hide their secret sins, they were scattered under a dark veil of forgetfulness, being horribly astonished and troubled by strange apparitions.

Neither did the den that held them protect them from fear, but instead, noises coming down sounded around them, and sad visions appeared to them, frightening them. No power of the fire could provide them with light, and neither could the bright flames of the stars lighten that horrible night. The only thing that appeared to them was a sudden dreadful fire that lit itself, and they were more terrified of that face than the sight they didn't see."

"The illusions of their magic were put down, and their bragging about their wisdom was tested and found disgraceful, for they who promised to drive away terrors and troubles from sick minds, were sick themselves from fear, and worthy to be laughed at. No terrible thing had attacked them, yet they became afraid of animals passing by and hissing snakes, and they died in fear, denying what they saw in the air, which could be in no way avoided. Wickedness is fearful and condemns herself through her testimony, as a troubled conscience always predicts terrible things. For fear is nothing else but an abandoning of the help that reason offers. While there is less expectation from within, it counts more than ignorance of the cause of the torment. But they sleeping the same sleep that night, which was indeed intolerable, and which came on them out of the bottoms of inevitable Hades, were partly vexed with monstrous visions and partly fainted as their heart failed them. A sudden unexpected fear came on them, so then whoever fell down there was immediately kept, locked up in a prison without iron bars. Whether he was a farmer, or shepherd, or a field worker, he was overtaken, and endured that necessity, which could not be avoided, for they were all bound with one chain of darkness."

"Whether it was a whistling wind, or a melodious noise of birds among the spreading branches, or a pleasing fall of violently running water, or a terrible sound of stones thrown down, or the thunder of beast running that could not be seen, or a roaring voice of most savage wild animals, or a rebounding echo from the hollow mountains, these things made them collapse in fear. The whole cosmos was lit with clear light, and none were hindered in their labor, yet over them only, was spread a heavy night, an image of that darkness which should afterward receive them, but were they themselves were more terrible than the darkness."

Wisdom of Solomon: Chapter 18

[Continued from the previous chapter,] "Nevertheless, your saints saw a very great light whose voice they heard, but they did not see their shape. Because they had praised you, they did not suffer the same way, and those who had been wronged before gave thanks and were not hurt. They begged them to pardon those who had been enemies. Instead, you gave them a burning pillar of fire, both to be a guide on the unknown journey and a harmless sun to entertain them honorably. They were worthy of being deprived of light and imprisoned in darkness, those who had kept your sons locked up, through whom the pure light of the law was to be given to the cosmos. When they had decided to kill the babes of the saints, one child was thrown away and saved to test them. You took away the multitude of their children and destroyed them altogether in a mighty water. That night was known before by our fathers, that assuredly knowing to what oaths they had trusted in, they might be of better courage."

"So your people received both the salvation of the just and destruction of their enemies. You punished our enemies the same way you glorified us, who you had called. The just children of good men sacrificed secretly and unanimously created a just Torah, that both could be partakers, both the good and evil, who now sing the praise of the Father. But on the other side, there came a terrible cry of the enemies, and sad noise was heard for children who were being mourned. The master and the servant were punished in the same way, everyone from the king to the common people. They all together had innumerable dead with one kind of death, and the living was not enough to bury them all, for in one moment all the firstborn of them were destroyed."

"Whereas before they would not believe anything, due to the enchantments that caused the destruction of the firstborn, they acknowledged these people to be the sons of God. While all things were quiet and the night was mid-course, your almighty words leaped down from the sky out of your royal throne, like a fierce warrior of destruction into the middle of the land, and brought your genuine commandment like a sharp sword. Standing up he filled all things with death, and he touched the sky, even those he stood on the Earth. Then suddenly visions and horrible dreams troubled them terribly, and terrors came on them suddenly. One thrown here, and another there, half-dead, showed the cause of his death. For the dreams that troubled them foreshadowed these things, so they didn't die and not know why they were punished."

"The tasting of death touched the just also, and there was a destruction of the multitude in the wilderness, but the anger did not last long. Then the blameless man rushed and stood before them to defend them, and brought the shield of his proper ministry, including prayer, and the appeasing with incense. He set himself against the anger, and so brought the calamity to an end, declaring that he was your servant. He overcame the destroyer, not with strength of body or force of arms, but with a word subdued him that punished, alleging the oaths and covenants made with the fathers. When the dead were now fallen down by heaps one on another, standing between the heaps he stayed the anger and parted the way for the living. For in the long garment was the whole cosmos, and on the four rows of the stones were the glory of the fathers engraved, and your majesty on the diadem of his head. To these, the destroyer gave place, and was afraid of them, for it was enough that they only tasted of the anger."

Wisdom of Solomon: Chapter 19

[Continued from the previous chapter,] "As for the unjust, anger came on them without mercy, as he knew what they would do. How, having given them leave to depart, and sent them quickly away, they would change their mind and chase them. While they were still mourning and lamenting at the graves of the dead, they did another foolish thing and chased them like fugitives, whom they had previously begged to leave. The destiny of which they were worthy, drew them to this end and made them forget the things that had already happened, so they might fulfill the punishment which was lacking in their torment. Your people might pass a wonderful way, but they might find a strange death. For the whole creature in his proper kind was fashioned again anew, serving the peculiar commandments that were given to them, that your children might be kept without pain."

A cloud shadowed the camp, and where water stood before, dry land appeared, and out of the Papyrus Sea, a way without hindrance, and out of the violent stream a green field appeared across which all the people traveled that were defended by your hand, and saw your marvelous and strange wonders. They who went fed like horses, and leaped like lambs, praising you, the Lord, who had saved them. They still remembered the things that were done while they stayed in the foreign land, and how the ground brought out flies instead of livestock, and how the river threw out a multitude of frogs instead of fish. Yet afterward, they saw a new generation of birds, when, being led by their appetite, they asked delicate meats, and quails came up to them from the sea for their contentment."

"Punishments came on the sinners, but not without the former signs. By the force of thunders, they suffered justly according to their own wickedness, as they were hard and hateful towards strangers. The Sodomites did not receive those who they did not know when they came, but these ones sold their guests into slavery when they had deserved better from them. Not only that, but in another respect, they were even worse, for the others against their will received the strangers, but these grievously punished those who they had received with celebration and were following the same laws as them."

"Therefore with blindness were these punished, as those were at the doors of the righteous man, when, being surrounded with horrible great darkness, everyone wanted the path to his own doors. The elements were changed in themselves by a kind of harmony, like as in a lute notes change the name of the tune, yet all continue to make sound, which may clearly be perceived by the very sight. Earthly things were turned into watery, and the things, that before swam in the water, now went on the ground. Fire had power in the water, forgetting his own virtue, and the water forgot his own quenching nature. On the other side, the flames did not consume the flesh of the corruptible living things, though they walked within it, it neither melted they the icy kind of heavenly meat that was its nature to melt. For in all things, Lord, you magnified your people and glorified them. You did not regard them lightly, but did assist them in every time and place."

Psalms of Solomon: Chapter 1

I cried to the Lord[1] when afflicted to the end, and to God[2] when sinners attacked. I heard the alarm of war, and I said, "He will listen to me, who seeks Sydyk."[3]

I thought in my heart that I was full of lawfulness because I was well off and had become rich in children. Their wealth spread to the whole earth, their glory to the ends of the earth. They were exalted to the stars, and they said they would never fall, but they became insolent in their prosperity, and they did not understand. They sinned in secret, and even I did not know of them. Their transgressions went beyond those of the heathens before them, and they completely defiled the holy things of the Lord.

Psalms of Solomon: Chapter 1 Notes

1 Septuagint manuscript 149: cyrion (ᴋυρ̄ιον). Translation: lord

Assuming the records of the translation of the Septuagint are correct, then the Psalms of Solomon was translated from an Aramaic text, which would have read either ådny (ᵓᵞᵞᴎ) or bôlå (ᴎᴸᵞᵞ) where the Greek translation has cyrion (κύριον). Both terms translate as "lord," "owner," or "master."

2 Septuagint manuscript 149: ton theon (ᴛοᴎ θ͞οᴎ). Translation: the god

If the Psalms of Solomon was translated from an Aramaic source, the word translated as God (Θεοῦ) would have been ålh (ﾧﾝﾝﾝ), the Aramaic word meaning god, and the Aramaic translation of El, recorded as An (✳) in Akkadian Cuneiform, îl (𒀭𒈗) in Ugaritic, ål (𐤋𐤀) in Phoenician, el (𐡋𐡀) in Samaritan, and el (אֵל) in Hebrew, the name of the highest God of the Canaanite pantheon.

3 Septuagint manuscript 149: hati eplêsthên dicaeosynês (οτι ϛπλησθην Ꙃικλιοσυνησ). Translation: that approaches (or is filled with) justice (or fairness)

In sections of the Septuagint that were also translated into Hebrew, dicaeosynên (δικαιοσύνην) and dicaeosynês (δικαιοσύνησ) were the translation used where the Leningrad Codex retains tzedek (צֶדֶק). In addition to being the Canaanite word for "justice," Sdq was also the name of the Canaanite god of justice, recorded in the Bronze Age as Sdq (𒍦𒄿𒌑𒆠) in Ugaritic, and in the Iron Age as Sdq (𐤑𐤃𐤒) in Phoenician. During the Classical Era, the Greeks translated the name as Sydyk (Συδυκ), and during the Roman occupation of Judea, the name Tzedek (צֶדֶק) was the Hebrew translation of the Roman god "Jupiter," and as such continues to be the Hebrew name of the planet Jupiter. In his 4th century AD work Praeparatio Evangelica, the Christian historian Eusebius of Caesarea, quoted Philo of Byblos' 2nd century AD translation of Sanchuniathon's Bronze Age Phoenician History, which reported that Misor and Sydyk were the Canaanite gods of equality and justice.

Psalms of Solomon: Chapter 2

A Psalm of Solomon about Jerusalem

When the sinner grew proud, he came with a battering ram and knocked down the fortified walls,[1] and you did not restrain him. Foreign nations ascended your altar, and they trampled it proudly with their sandals, because the sons of Jerusalem had defiled the holy things of the Lord, and had profaned with iniquities the offerings to God. Therefore he said, "Take them far from me!"

It was seen as nothing by God, and it was completely dishonored. The sons and the daughters were in terrible captivity, with shackles around their necks, branded as slaves among the nations.[2] According to their sins, he has repaid them, for he has left them in the hands of those who conquered them. He has turned away his face from pitying them, young and old and their children all together, for they had done evil one and all, in not listening. Shamayim[3] was angry and Eretz[4] hated them, for no man on the land had done what they had done, and Eretz knew the judgment of Misor the god.[5] They set the sons of Jerusalem to be mocked at, in return for the prostitutes in her. Every traveler entered during the full light of the day. They mocked with their transgressions, as they themselves were used to doing. In the full light of the day, they revealed their iniquities. The daughters of Jerusalem were defiled in accordance with your judgment because they had defiled themselves with unnatural intercourse.

I am pained in my bowels and my inward parts for these things. Yet, I consider you right, God, in uprightness of heart! For in your judgments is your lawfulness displayed, God. For you have repaid the sinners according to their deeds, yes, according to their very wicked sins. You have exposed their sins, so your judgment might be manifest! You have wiped out their memory from the Earth. God judges fairly and does not admire individuals.

For the nations insulted Jerusalem, trampled it down, and her beauty was dragged down from the glorious throne. She dressed in sackcloth instead of beautiful clothing, a rope was around her head instead of a crown. She took off the glorious crown which God had set on her and dishonorably was her beauty thrown to the ground.

I saw and begged the Lord and said, "Long enough, Lord has your hand been heavy against Israel, in bringing the nations against them. They have ridiculed us mercilessly in fierce anger, and they will completely annihilate us, unless you, Lord, rebuke them in your anger. They have done it not in zeal, but in the lust of the mind,[6] pouring out their anger on us with an intent to plunder. Don't delay, God, to repay them, and to turn the pride of the dragon[7] into dishonor."

I did not wait long before God showed me that the insolent one had been slain in the mountains[8] of Egypt, considered of less account than the lowest, on land and sea. His body, too, was carried here and there on the billows with much insolence, and with none to bury him, because he had rejected him with dishonor.

He thought that he was not a man, and did not consider that he would die. He said, "I will be lord of land and sea, and he did not recognize that it is God who is great, and mighty in his great strength. He is king over the skies and judges kings and kingdoms. It is he who set me up in glory and brought down the proud to eternal destruction in dishonor because they did not know him.

Now see, you princes of the Earth, the judgment of the Lord, for he is a great king, and righteously judges all who are under the sky. Bless God, you who wisely fear the Lord, for the mercy of the Lord will be on those who fear him, in the judgment. He will distinguish between the lawful and the sinner, repay the sinners forever according to their deeds, and have mercy on the lawful, delivering him from the affliction of the sinner, and repaying the sinner for what he has done to the lawful. For the Lord is good to those that call on him in patience, doing according to his mercy to his pious ones, and establishing them for all time before him with his strength.

May the Lord be praised by his servants forever!

Psalms of Solomon: Chapter 2 Notes

1 This line about the walls of Jerusalem being destroyed is often used to date the text, however, the walls of Jerusalem were not recorded as being torn down during the time of King Solomon. Pharaoh Necho II occupied the city circa 609 BC and destroyed its fortifications. The Babylonians destroyed the city entirely in 587 BC, and so that could not be the incident in question. The Persians appeared to have occupied the city without opposition in 525 BC, as they did not record a siege of the city as they recorded for other sites in Phoenicia.

Nehemiah reported that the city's walls had been destroyed shortly before he traveled to Jerusalem in 384 BC. Jerusalem surrendered to Alexander's forces in 332 BC without a siege, and the Greeks did not record the city's walls being torn down. General Pompey tore down the walls of Jerusalem after occupying the city in 63 BC, as described in Josephus' The Wars of the Jews, and this is generally accepted as being the event in question, which would place the composition of Chapters 1 and 2 to after 63 BC. Alternatively, if the event in question was Necho II's occupation of Jerusalem, or whatever happened in the time of Nehemiah, it would date the composition of chapters 1 and 2 to anytime after 609 BC.

2 The reference to the Israelites being taken away as slaves is often used to date the composition of Chapters 1 and 2, however, Israelites, like all conquered peoples, were often taken as slaves after battles that they lost. The ten tribes of Samaria were taken away as slaves after the Assyrians conquered Samaria in 720 BC. The Egyptians would have taken Judahites as slaves in 609 BC, after conquering Judea. The Babylonians took Judahites as slaves in 587 BC, and they were reportedly freed by the Persians in 539 BC. There were a large number of Judeans were taken as slaves by Ptolemy I Soter of Egypt during the wars between the successors of Alexander, circa 320 BC. General Pompey also took Jewish slaves after occupying the city in 63 BC.

3 Septuagint manuscript 149: Ouranos (Ουρ̆ἀνοσ).

Translations: Uranus (or sky)

The Septuagint used the translation of Uranus (Οὐρανὸσ) where the Masoretic texts retain Shamayim (שָׁמַיִם), the name of the ancient Canaanite god of the sky. The "army of Shamayim" was worshiped by the early Israelites until King Josiah's reforms circa 625 BC, indicating the Psalms of Solomon were likely composed before King Josiah, or by Samaritans before 69 BC, who were not concerned with Josiah's reforms until after the reconstitution of Samaritanism during the Herodian Dynasty. As the text is referencing a god or spirit, the Hebrew name Shamayim is used in this translation.

4 Septuagint manuscript 149: Gê (ⲅⲏ). Translation: Ge (or land, earth, country, soil)

The Septuagint used the translation of Gê (Γῆ) where the Masoretic texts retain aretz (אֶרֶץ), more commonly transliterated as Eretz, the name of the ancient Canaanite goddess of the Earth, or Adamah (אֲדָמָה), the Edomite goddess of the Earth. The goddess Eretz continued to be worshiped by Israelites until the Greco-Roman era, and without knowing if this was originally Eretz or Adama, it cannot be used to date the text. As the text is referencing a god or spirit, the Hebrew name Eretz is used in this translation, as it is more common in the Masoretic texts than Adama.

5 Septuagint manuscript 149: dicaea ho theos (ⲇⲓⲕⲁⲓⲁ ⲟ ⲑⲉⲟⲥ). Translation: equal (or fairness, balanced, righteous) the god

In addition to being the Canaanite word for "fairness" (𐤌𐤔𐤓), Misor was also the name of the Canaanite god of fairness and appears to be what the Greeks translated as dicaea (δίκαια) in this verse. The god Misor was no longer worshiped by Israelites by the end of the Persian Era, likely due to the similarity with the Zoroastrian god Ahura Mazda, and therefore, was translated several ways by the Greeks, including hosiotêti (ὁσιότητι) in Wisdom of Solomon. The name was also transliterated as Misôr (Μισωρ) in some places, notably in Joshua, where it was the name of a village named after the god.

Misor and Sydyk were treated as a pair of gods throughout early Semitic history. The earliest surviving mention of the pair of gods is believed to be Mešar and Išar recorded in the Mari Cuneiform tablets from the 3rd millennium BC. The Mari Cuneiform tablets are from the ancient city of Mari, on the Euphrates River in eastern modern Syria. The tablets are written in a different language from the Akkadian Cuneiform tablets found in the territory of modern Iraq, however, used the same symbols. Depending on the translator, they are interpreted as an early form of the Canaanite language, a precursor to the Aramaic language, or another Semitic language separate from both the Western and Eastern Semitic language branches. However the language is interpreted, the gods Mešar and Išar as accepted as early versions of Misor and Sydyk, which then also means the Akkadian equivalents of Mešar and Išar, recorded as Misharu and Kittu, are the Akkadian equivalents of Misor and Sydyk.

6 Septuagint manuscript 149: psychên (Ψυχλν).

Translation: mind, personality, psyche
Hebrew equivalent in other books: nefesh (נֶפֶשׁ).
Translation: mind, life, soul, person

7 Septuagint manuscript 149: dracontos (ΑβΔιοντοσ).

Translation: dragon

The Greeks translated both tannin (תַּנִּין), meaning "crocodiles," and "Livyatan" (לִוְיָתָן), the name of the constellation Cetus, as "dragon" (δράκοντος) in the Septuagint. Both terms are derived from Canaanite and are found in the Ugaritic texts as tnn (►►►►►►), the word meaning crocodile, and Ltn (ΙΙΙ►►►►), the name of the asterism now known as Cetus. Both terms were used as metaphors for the enemies of the Lord in the Israelite religions, as Judge Lotan was another name for Lord Yam, who was the enemy of Ba'al in the Ugaritic texts. Both the prophets Isaiah and Ezekiel referred to Egypt as tannin, and as it was to the south of Judah, it was viewed as being governed by Cetus (Leviathan) by followers of the Neo-Babylonian and Persian era followers of the Judahite star cults, who also viewed Dobiel (Ursa Major) as the constellation governing the Persians, who were from the north.

8 Septuagint manuscript 149: oreôn (οῤόων). Translation: mountains

While there are mountains in Egypt, the reference is nevertheless odd without knowing the context of the story. Modern historians generally assume it is the story of the Roman General Pompey sacking Jerusalem 63 BC, and this may be correct, however, it could equally be applied to Pharaoh Necho II's sack of Jerusalem in 609 BC. Pharaoh Necho II was the first Egyptian King to develop a national navy, by hiring Greek sailors, as Egyptians were notoriously scared of the open sea. This would explain why the author of this psalm made a point of saying the dragon wanted to be "lord of land and sea," which would have been an irrelevant statement about a Roman General, as, by that era, all countries had national navies.

As both men died in Egypt, the psalm could be about either, however, the reference to the 'mountains' of Egypt, makes more sense as a translation error of "deserts of Egypt," which could have only happened if the initial report of the death of the "dragon" reached Jerusalem in Demotic, the official script of Egypt between 650 and 400 BC. In Demotic, "mountain" and "desert" are spelled identically, as tŭ (ʃ⁻). It is not known if Necho II died in a desert or a mountain, however, Pompey certainly did not die in either, he was executed in Alexandria, on the Mediterranean coast.

Psalms of Solomon: Chapter 3

A Psalm of Solomon about the lawful[1]

Why do you sleep, my mind, and do not praise the Lord? Sing a new song to the god who is worthy to be praised! Sing, and be quick before he awakes, as it is good to sing psalms to God from a happy heart.

The lawful remember the Lord at all times, with thanksgiving and declaration of the lawfulness of the Lord's judgments.

The lawful doesn't despise the punishments of the Lord, as his will is always before the Lord.

The lawful stumbles and grasps for the Lord of lawfulness. If he falls, he looks out for what God will do to him and searches for a way in which his deliverance may come.

The lawful hold steadfast to God, their salvation.

In the house of the lawful, there is no room for sin compounded by sin.

The lawful constantly searches his house, to remove all iniquity he has done by accident. He makes atonement for sins of ignorance by fasting and afflicting his mind, the Lord counts guiltless every pious man and his house.

The sinner stumbles and curses his life and the day when he was fathered, and his mother's labor.

He adds sins to sins while he lives, and when he falls, terrible is his fall, and he will not rise again.

The destruction of the sinner is forever, and he will not be remembered when the lawful is visited.

This is the reward of sinners forever.

Yet those who fear the Lord will rise to eternal life, and their life will be in the light of the Lord, and will never end.

Psalms of Solomon: Chapter 3 Notes

1 Septuagint manuscript 149: dicaeôn (ＤＩＬ.Δlooν). Translation: "the lawful people"

This is often interpreted as a reference to the Pharisees, however, it is more likely a reference to the Essenes, who followed their Torah more strictly than the Pharisees followed Moses' Torah. It is clear from Josephus' description that they were not practicing a recognized form of Judaism, however, were descended from known Israelite families, and were therefore "Jews by birth," while Philo of Alexandria reported that believed their ancestors were Canaanites and not Israelites.

They are likely the Nazarite sect mentioned in 1st Maccabees, and the Nazarenes from the time of John the

Baptist, who abstained from animal flesh other than fish and birds, both of which are mentioned along with plants as the food 'for every living thing' in chapter 5. Both the Aramaic term Nazarite and Greek term Nazarene are derived from the Hebrew word nzyr (נזיר), which translates as "separate" or "consecrated" and refers to people strictly adhering to the laws of the Torah and the Talmud in Rabbinical Judaism. The term first appeared in the Book of Judges implying it was an old term within the Israelite religions, however, its meaning is not clearly defined within Judaism before the Talmud, composed between 200 and 800 AD.

In the Book of Judges, generally regarded as the oldest surviving Israelite text that had not been heavily redacted, Samson was listed as a Nazarite from birth, and was prohibited from drinking alcohol, eating meat, or cutting his hair, none of which is found in the surviving laws of Moses, suggesting a different Torah was being used by the Nazarites at the beginning of the Iron Age.

Psalms of Solomon: Chapter 4

A Dialog of Solomon about the man-pleasers

Why do you sit, you profane man, in the council of the pious, considering that your heart is far removed from the Lord, provoking with transgressions the god of Israel?[1] Extravagant in speech, and extravagant in outward appearance beyond all men, is he who severely condemns the sinners in his judgments. His hand is first against them as though he acts in zeal, yet he is himself guilty of many sins, and greed. His eyes are on every woman without distinction, and his tongue lies when he contracts through an oath. At night he sins in secret as though unseen, with his eyes he talks to every woman of sinful arrangements. He is quick to enter every house cheerfully, as though he were guileless.

Let God remove the hypocrites from the company of the pious, and take the life of such a one through disease and poverty. Let God reveal the deeds of the man-pleasers, and the deeds of them with laughter and derision, so that the pious may view the judgment of their God as righteous, when sinners are removed from the lawful, even from the man-pleasers who skillfully speak the law.

Their eyes are fixed on any man's house which is still secure, so they might, like a serpent, destroy the wisdom [...missing text...] through the words of transgression. His words are deceitful so he may accomplish his wicked desire. He never stops from scattering families as though they were orphans, yes, he lays waste to a house on account of his lawless desire. He deceives with words, saying, "There is none that sees or judges."

He fills one house with lawlessness, then his eyes are fixed on the next house to destroy it with words that give wing to desire. Yet with all these, his mind, like Sheol,[2] is not sated. Let him, Lord, be dishonored before you. Let him go out groaning, and come home cursed. Let his life be spent in anguish, poverty, and need, Lord! Let his sleep be troubled with pains and his awaking with confusion. Let sleep be withdrawn from his eyelids at night, and let him dishonorably fail in every work of his hands. Let him return empty-handed to his house, and his house be void of everything which he could sate his appetite. Let his old age be spent in childless loneliness until death takes him.

Let the flesh of the man-pleasers be ripped apart by wild animals! Let the bones of the lawless lie dishonored in the sight of Shemesh.[3] Let ravens peck out the eyes of the hypocrites. For they have laid waste to many houses of men, and in dishonor scattered them in their lust. They have not remembered God, nor were afraid of God in all these things, but they have provoked God's anger and troubled him. May he remove them from the Earth, because with deceit they beguiled the minds of the flaw-less.

Blessed are they that fear the Lord in their flawless-ness, the Lord will deliver them from guileful men and sinners, deliver us from every stumbling block of the lawless. Let God destroy those who insolently work all unlawfulness, for a great and mighty judge is the Lord our lawful god.

Let your mercy, Lord, be on all those who love you!

Psalms of Solomon: Chapter 4 Notes

1 Septuagint manuscript 149: theon Israêl (θεον ιϲραηλ).

Translation: god Israel

The term theon Israêl (θεὸν Ισραηλ) is found throughout the Septuagint, generally matched by the term ȧlhy yšrȧl (אלהי ישראל) in the Masoretic texts, both of which translate as "god Israel." It is a convention to insert "of" between the words, changing the term to term to "god of Israel," however, both Greek and Hebrew had terms that meant "of," suggesting that Israel may have originally been viewed as the god's name or title. If so, that would precede the composition of the story of Jacob being renamed Israel in the Torah, and the stories of Isaac being renamed Israel in the other ancient Israelite text.

2 Septuagint manuscript 149: hadês (ܐܝܠܗܣ)

Hades was the fiery Greek underworld, which was adopted by Christians, Buddhists, and some Jews in the pre-Christian era. The term Hades is used in the Septuagint where the Masoretic texts use Šåůl (שאול), which, based on the earlier description of the "land of perpetual darkness" in the book of Job, cannot have originally been a reference to the Greek fiery underworld, but something like the Erṣetu (𒌨𒆠𒅅𒈨𒍦) of the Babylonians. The traditional Canaanite land of the dead was Mirey (𒌋𒈨𒊑), the land ruled by Mot the god of the dead, who was later seen by the ancient Hebrews as the messenger of death according to the books of Habakkuk, Hosea, and Jeremiah.

3 Septuagint manuscript 149: Hêliou (Ηλιου). Translation: Helios (or sun)

The Septuagint uses the translation of Helios ('Ηλίου), the Greek god of the sun, where the Aleppo Codex retains the name Shemesh (שמש), the Canaanite god of the sun, as well as the word for sun. The worship of Shemesh was banned by King Josiah of Judah circa 625 BC, along with the worship of the Moon, Lord (Ba'al), Asherah, and stars (armies of the sky). The author of 1st Ezra claimed that after killing King Josiah, King Necho II of Egypt restored the worship of the Lord in Jerusalem, and as Necho was a sun worshiper, recorded in the Egyptian records as worshiping the southern Egyptian sun god Amen, and the northern Egyptian sun-god Atum, the lord whose worship he restored in Jerusalem had to have been Shemesh. When Necho killed Josiah, he placed King Jehoiakim on the throne of Judah, who, according to the Talmud, claimed the only thing that God provided the world with was light, proving that he too was a sun-worshiper. During Jehoiakim's reign, Jeremiah, a Yahwist prophet from the Levites of Libnah, and the architect of King Josiah's reforms was imprisoned in the royal prison as a heretic until the Babylonians destroyed Jerusalem in 587 BC. Five years later, while a captive in Babylon, Jeremiah's scribe Baruch also described his god as being the sun and claimed that his sacred name was Amen, proving that the Judahites taken captive to Babylon were also worshiping the sun, as the Babylonians and Egyptians were at the time.

This psalm's reference to the 'sight of the Sun' implies the author viewed the Sun as a god, but not God. This would place the composition of this verse in the early Persian era at the latest, as sun worship appears to have disappeared from Judah by the late Persian era.

Psalms of Solomon: Chapter 5

A Psalm of Solomon

The god Lord, I will praise your name with joy, among those that know your righteous judgments. As you are good and merciful, the refuge of the poor. When I cry to you, do not silently ignore me, for no man takes plunder from a mighty man. Who, then, can take anything of which you have made, except that which you give? For man and his portion lie before you in the balance. He cannot add to it and enlarge what has been prescribed by you.

God, when we are in distress we call on you for help, and you do not reject our petition, for you are our God. Don't cause your hand to be heavy on us, in case through necessity we sin. Even though you don't restore us, we will not keep away, but to you will we come. If I hunger, to you will I cry, God, and you will provide for me.

You feed the birds and fish,[1] in that you give rain to the land that green plants may grow up, and so create food in the land for every living thing. If they hunger, to you they lift up their face. Kings and rulers and peoples you nourish, God, so who is the help of the poor and needy, if not you, Lord? You will listen, as who is good and gentle like you? Make the mind of the humiliated happy by opening your merciful hand.

Man's goodness is bestowed grudgingly and [...missing text...] If he repeats it without murmuring, even that is marvelous. But your gift is great in goodness and wealth, he trusts in you and has no lack of gifts. Throughout the whole Earth is your mercy in goodness, Lord.

Happy is he who God remembers and grants to him due sufficiency. If a man gains too much, he sins. The lawful are sufficient with moderate means, and hereby the blessing of the Lord becomes an abundance with lawfulness. They that fear the Lord rejoice in good gifts, your goodness is on Israel in your kingdom.

Blessed is the Glorious Lord, for he is our king!

Psalms of Solomon: Chapter 5 Notes

1 The reference to the "fish and birds," along with plants as the food "for every living thing," implies that this Psalm was written by a Nazarene, as they abstained from animal flesh other than fish and birds. It also suggests that the Psalms of Solomon were a Nazarene collection of songs, which would be consistent with both John 'the Baptist' and his cousin Jesus 'the Nazarene' being executed when their followers claimed they were descended from King Solomon, and therefore were the rightful kings of Judea. Most of these psalms embrace a rejection of material wealth and refer to the adherents as the lawful (sometimes translated as righteous) or the pious. According to Josephus' description of the Essenes, they rejected money and wealth and followed their Torah more strictly than the Jews followed the Torah of Moses.

The connection between the Essenes and Nazarenes is generally debated among scholars, as so far, there is not enough evidence to conclusively prove the Nazarenes were an Essene sect, however, the circumstantial evidence is in favor of the connection. Unfortunately, as John the Baptist was a Nazarene, and Jesus was baptized by him, it raises significant questions within Christian interpretations of the Old Testament that few churches want to deal with, and so Christian scholars generally dismiss the reported similarities of the groups as coincidence. Likewise, Rabbinical Jews have little interest in a heretical group of non-practicing Jews, and so generally ignore them entirely, although Jewish scholars do accept the connection between the Essenes, Nazarenes, and earliest Christians, as it does not raise any questions within their faith. Most of the research into the connection between these groups has been done at non-religious institutes in the past few decades since the Dead Sea Scrolls became available for study.

Psalms of Solomon: Chapter 6

'Of Trust,' by Solomon

Happy is the man whose heart is fixed on calling on the name of the Lord. When he remembers the name of the Lord, he will be saved. His path is made by the Lord, and the works of his hands are preserved by the Lord his god. His mind will not be troubled by what he sees in nightmares. When he passes through rivers and the waves of the seas, he will not be dismayed. He arises from his sleep and blesses the name of the Lord. His heart is at peace, and he sings to the name of his god. He begs the Lord for all his house, and the Lord hears the prayer of everyone who fears God. Every request of the mind that hopes in him, the Lord accomplishes.

Blessed is the Lord, who shows mercy to those who love him sincerely.

Psalms of Solomon: Chapter 7

'Of Returning,' by Solomon

Don't stay far from us, God, in case those who hate us attack us without cause. You have rejected them, God, so don't let their feet trample on your holy inheritance. Chasten us yourself as you will, but don't give us up to the nations, for, if you send pestilence, you yourself give it orders about us, for you are merciful, and will not be angry to the point of destroying us. While your name lives among us, we will find mercy, and the nations will not prevail against us. You are our shield when we call on you, and you listen to us. You will pity the seed of Israel forever and you will not reject them, but we will be under your yoke forever, under the rod of your punishment. You will establish us when you help us, showing mercy to the house of Jacob on the day in which you promised to help them.

Psalms of Solomon: Chapter 8

'Of the Musician,' by Solomon

My ears have heard distress and the sounds of war. The sound of a trumpet announcing slaughter and calamity. The sound of many people, like an extremely fast wind, like a mighty firestorm sweeping through the Negev. I said in my heart, "Certainly God is judging us!"

I heard a sound moving towards Jerusalem, the holy city, and my loins were broken at what I heard. My knees shook, and my heart was afraid, my bones were dismayed like flax. I said, "They establish their ways in lawfulness."

I thought about the judgments of God since the creation of the sky and earth, and I saw God righteous in his judgments which have been from ancient times. God saw their sins in the full light of the day, and all the earth came to know the lawful judgments of God. In secret places underground, their iniquities were committed to provoke him to anger, and they worked perversion, son with mother and father with daughter. They committed adultery, every man with his neighbor's wife. They concluded covenants with one another, with oaths covering these things.

They plundered the sanctuary of God, as though there was no avenger. They stepped the altar of the Lord, coming straight from all manner of uncleanness. With menstrual blood, they defiled the sacrifices, as though these were common flesh. They left no sin undone, in which they surpassed the heathens. Therefore God created for them a spirit of wandering and gave them a cup of undiluted wine to drink, so they might become drunk.

He brought him from the edge of the earth, who struck mightily, and he decreed war against Jerusalem, and against her land. The princes of the land went to meet him with joy, and they said to him, "Blessed be your way! Come, enter in peace."

They made the rough ways even, before his entering in, and they opened the gates to Jerusalem and crowned its walls. Like a father entered the house of his sons, so he entered Jerusalem in peace, and he occupied it in great safety. He captured her fortresses and the wall of Jerusalem, for God himself led him in safety, while they wandered. He destroyed their princes and every one wise in counsel, and he poured out the blood of the inhabitants of Jerusalem like unclean water. He led away their sons and daughters, who they had fathered in defilement. They did according to their uncleanness, even as their fathers had done. They defiled Jerusalem and the things that had been sacred to the name of God.

Yet God has shown himself righteous in his judgments on the nations of the Earth. The pious servants of God are like innocent lambs in their midst. The Lord that judges the whole earth in his lawfulness is worthy to be praised. See, now, God, you have shown us your judgment in your lawfulness. Our eyes have seen your judgments, God, and we have justified your name which is honored forever. You are the God of lawfulness, judging Israel with punishment.

Turn your mercy on us, and pity us, God! Gather together the dispersed people of Israel, with mercy and goodness. For your faithfulness is with us, and though we have stiffened our necks, yet you are our punisher. Don't overlook us, our god, in case the nations swallow us up, as though there were none to save us. You are our god from the beginning and in you our trust set, Lord. We will not leave you, for your judgments are good to us. Ours and our children's is your good pleasure forever, Lord, our savior, and we will never again be removed. The Lord is worthy to be praised for his judgments with the mouths of his pious ones.

Blessed be Israel by the Lord forever!

Psalms of Solomon: Chapter 9

'For Rebuke' by Solomon

When Israel was led away captive into a strange land, and when they fell away from the Lord who redeemed them? They were thrown away from the inheritance, which the Lord had given them. The Israelites were dispersed among every nation according to the word of God, that you might be justified, God, in your lawfulness because of our transgressions. You are a just judge over all the peoples of the Earth. None who does unjustness is hidden from your knowledge, and the lawful deeds of your pious ones are before you, Lord. Where, then, can a man hide from your knowledge, God? Our works are subject to our own choice and power to do right or wrong in the works of our hands. In your lawfulness, you visited the sons of men. He who does lawfulness lays up life for himself with the Lord, and he who does wrongly forfeits his life to destruction.

The judgments of the Lord are given in lawfulness to every man and his house. To whom are you good, God, except to those that call on the Lord? He cleanses from sins a mind when it confesses when it makes acknowledgment. Shame is on us and shows on our faces because of all these things.

Whose sins does he forgive, except to those who have sinned? You blessed the lawful, and do not reprove them for the sins that they have committed. Your goodness is on those who sin when they repent. And, now, you are our god, and we are the people whom you have loved. Look and show pity, God of Israel, for we are yours. Do not remove your mercy from us, in case they attack us. For you chose the descendants of Abraham before all the nations and set your name on us, Lord. You will not reject us forever. You made a covenant with our fathers concerning us, and we trust in you, when our mind turns to you.

May the mercy of the Lord be on the Temple of Israel forever and ever!

Psalms of Solomon: Chapter 10

A Song of Solomon

Happy is the man who the Lord remembers with reproving, who he restrains from the way of evil with strokes, so he may be cleansed from sin and it may not be multiplied. He who prepares his back for strokes will be cleansed, for the Lord is good to those who endure the punishment. He makes straight the ways of the lawful and does not pervert them through his punishment. The mercy of the Lord is on those who love him honestly, the Lord remembers his servants in mercy.

The testimony is in the Torah[1] of the eternal covenant, the testimony of the Lord is on the ways of men in his visitation. Just and kind is our Lord in his judgments, forever Israel will praise the name of the Lord in joy. The pious will give thanks in the assembly of the people, God will have mercy on the poor and in the joy of Israel, for good and merciful is God forever, and the assemblies of Israel will glorify the name of the Lord.

May the salvation of the Lord be in the house of Israel forever in joy!

Psalms of Solomon: Chapter 10 Notes

1 Septuagint manuscript 149: nomos (ﬡﬡμοσ). Translation: usage, custom, law, ordinance, melody, song)

The Greek word nomos (νόμοσ) was adopted into Aramaic as nmůså (ﬡﬡﬡﬡ), meaning "law" or "ordinance," supporting the Greek translation of "Torah" as nomos. This verse is refers to events in Cosmic Genesis, which means this verse must have either been composed after Cosmic Genesis became part of the Torah, or, by someone following the older Israelite religion that originally created Cosmic Genesis. As most of Cosmic Genesis appears to have been written in Aramaic, and the book draws on both Akkadian and Hurrian mythology, it was likely written in Aram, which was recorded as being part of Solomon's United Kingdom of Israel, as well as the later kingdom of Samaria, the short-lived Aramean Empire, the Neo-Assyrian Empire, Neo-Babylonian Empire, and finally the Persian Empire, before being conquered by Alexander the Great.

Psalms of Solomon: Chapter 11

'The Expectation,' by Solomon

Blow on the trumpet to summon the saints, you in Zion. Cause the voice of him that brings good news to be heard in Jerusalem, for God has had pity on Israel in visiting them. Stand in the heights of Jerusalem, and see your children from the east and the west, gathered together by the Lord, and from the north, they come in the joy of their god. From the faraway islands, God has gathered them.

High mountains have been knocked down, creating a plain for them. The hills fled at their entrance. The woods sheltered them as they passed by, and every sweet-smelling tree, God caused to spring up for them, so Israel might pass by in the visitation of the glory of their God. Put on your glorious garments Jerusalem, and prepare your holy robe, for God has spoken good things concerning Israel forever and ever. Let the Lord do what he has stated concerning Israel and Jerusalem. Let the Lord elevate Israel in his glorious name.

The mercy of the Lord is on Israel forever and ever!

Psalms of Solomon: Chapter 12

'Against the tongue of the transgressor,' by Solomon

Lord, deliver my mind from the lawless and wicked man, from the tongue that is lawless and slanderous and speaks lies and deceit. Many twisted words come from the tongue of the wicked man, and even among a people, a fire burns up their beauty. He delights to fill houses with a lying tongue, to cut down the trees of gladness which set on fire transgressors, and to involve households in warfare through slanderous lips.

May God remove the innocent far from the lips of transgressors by reducing them to need. May the bones of slanderers be scattered far away from those who fear the Lord! May the slanderous tongue perish in flaming fire far away from the pious! May the Lord preserve the quiet mind that hates the unrighteous. May the Lord establish the man that is in peace at home. The salvation of the Lord is on Israel his servant forever, and let the sinners perish together in the presence of the Lord. Yet, let the Lord's pious ones inherit the promises of the Lord.

Psalms of Solomon: Chapter 13

'Comfort for the lawful,' a Psalm by Solomon

The right hand of the Lord has covered me, and the right hand of the Lord has spared us. The arm of the Lord has saved us from the sword that passed through, and from famine and the death of sinners. Offensive animals ran at them, and with their teeth, they tore their flesh, with their molars crushed their bones. From all these things the Lord delivered us. The lawful was troubled on account of his errors, in case he should be taken away along with the sinners, for terrible is the downfall of the sinner, but not one of all these things touched the lawful.

The punishment of the lawful for sins done in ignorance is not the same as the overthrowing of the sinners. The lawful are punished secretly, in case the sinner rejoices over the lawful. He corrects the lawful as a beloved son. His punishment is like that of a firstborn. For the Lord spares his pious ones and erases their errors through his punishment. For the life of the lawful will be forever, but sinners will be taken away into destruction. Their memory will never be found again, but on the pious is the mercy of the Lord, and on those that fear him is his mercy.

Psalms of Solomon: Chapter 14

A Song of Solomon

The Lord is faithful to those who love him honestly, to those who endure his punishment, and to those who follow the lawfulness of his commandments in the Torah he commanded us that we might live. The lawful of the Lord will live by it forever in the paradise of the Lord. Among the trees of life, are his lawful ones, and their plants are rooted forever, they will not be plucked up all the days under the sky, for the portion and the inheritance of God is Israel.

But not so are the sinners and transgressors, who love the brief day spent in companionship with their sin. Their delight is in fleeting corruption, and they forget God. Yet, the ways of men are known to him at all times, and he knows the secrets of the heart before they happen. Therefore their inheritance is Sheol and darkness and destruction They will not be found on the day when the lawful obtain mercy, but the pious of the Lord will inherit life in gladness.

Psalms of Solomon: Chapter 15

'With a Song,' a Psalm by Solomon

When I was in distress I called on the name of the Lord, and I hoped for the help of the god of Jacob, and was saved.

The trust and refuge of the poor are you, God! Who has strength, except those who honestly give thanks to you, God? Through what is a man powerful, except through giving thanks to your name with a new psalm, sung with a joyful heart? The fruit of the lips with the well-tuned instrument of the tongue, and the first fruits of the lips from a pious and righteous heart. He who offers these things will never be shaken by evil, and the flame of fire and the anger against the unrighteous will not touch him, when it goes out from the face of the Lord against sinners, to consume all the flesh of sinners, as the mark of God is on the lawful that they may be saved.

Famine, sword, and pestilence will be far from the lawful, for they will flee from the lawful like men chased in war, yet they will pursue sinners and catch up to them. Those who are lawless will not escape the judgment of God. They will be surrounded as if by enemies experienced in war, as the mark of destruction is on their forehead. The inheritance of sinners is destruction and darkness, and their iniquities will chase them to

Sheol below. Their children will not find their inheritance, for sins will lay waste to the houses of sinners. Sinners will perish forever on the day of the Lord's judgment when God visits the Earth with his judgment. Yet they who fear the Lord will find mercy and will live through the compassion of their god. Nevertheless, sinners will perish forever!

Psalms of Solomon: Chapter 16

'Help for the Pious,' a Song of Solomon

When my mind slumbered and was far from the Lord, I had all but slipped down to the pit. When I was far from God, my mind had been well-near poured out to death, and I had been near the gates of Sheol with the sinner. When my mind departed from the Lord, the god in Israel, did not the Lord help me with his everlasting mercy?

He spurred me on, like a horse is spurred, that I might serve him, my savior and helper, at all times, who saved me. I will give thanks to you, God, for you have helped me to my salvation, and have not counted me with sinners to my destruction. Don't remove your mercy from me, God, nor your memory from my heart until I die. Rule me, God, keeping me back from wicked sin, from every wicked woman that causes the simple to stumble. Don't let the beauty of a lawless woman beguile me, nor anyone that is subject to unprofitable sin.

Establish the works of my hands before you, and preserve my actions in your memory. Protect my tongue and my lips with words of truth, and keep anger and irrational anger far from me. Remove the afflictions of murmuring and impatience from me. When I sin, punish me so I may return to you. But support my mind with goodwill and cheerfulness when you strengthen my mind. Make what is given to me be enough for me, for if you give not strength, who can endure punishment with poverty? When a man is rebuked through disease, your testing of him is in his flesh and the affliction of poverty.

If the lawful endures in all these trials, he will receive mercy from the Lord.

Psalms of Solomon: Chapter 17

'Song of the King,' a Psalm by Solomon.

Lord! You are our king forever and ever, for you, God, our minds praise.

How long are the days of man's life on the earth? As many as his days are, so is his trust set on him, but we trust in God, our savior, for the might of our God is forever merciful. The kingdom of our God rules forever over the nations in judgment.

You, Lord, chose David to be king over Israel and swore to him regarding his descendants, that never should his kingdom fail before you. Yet, due to our sins, sinners rose against us, and they attacked us and drove us out. What you had not promised to them, they took away from us with violence. They in no way praised your honorable name. They accepted a worldly monarchy in place of he who was their excellency. They laid waste to the throne of David in tumultuous arrogance. But you, God, threw them down, and removed their seed from the Earth, in that there rose up against them a man who was foreign to our race. According to their sins, you repaid them, God, so that it happened to them according to their actions.

God showed them no pity. He searched for their descendants and didn't let one of them go free. Faithful is the Lord in all his judgments which he does on the

Earth. The lawless ones laid waste to our land so that none inhabited it. They destroyed young and old and their children together. In the heat of his anger, he sent them away to the West, and he exposed the rulers of the land unsparingly to derision. Being a foreigner, the enemy acted proudly, and his heart was foreign from our god. He did all things in Jerusalem, as the people in the cities do to their gods.

The children of the covenant mingled among the peoples and surpassed them in evil. There was not among them one that worked in Jerusalem mercy and truth. Those who loved the synagogues of the pious fled from them, like sparrows that fly from their nest. They wandered in deserts so that their lives might be saved from harm, precious in the eyes of those who lived abroad was any that escaped alive from them. Over the whole Earth, they were scattered by lawless men. For the sky stopped the rain from falling on the Earth, and springs were stopped that flowed perennially out of the deeps, or that ran down from lofty mountains.

For there was none among those who worked lawfulness and justice, from the chief of them to the least of them, all were sinful. The king was a transgressor, the judge was disobedient, and the people were sinful.

Lord, see and raise for them their king, the son of David, at the time in which you choose, God, that he may reign over Israel your servants. Surround him with strength, that he may shatter unrighteous rulers, and that he may purge Jerusalem from nations that trample her down into destruction. In just wisdom, he will drive out sinners from the inheritance, and he will shatter the pride of the sinner like a potter's vessel. With an iron staff, he will break into pieces all their substance. He will destroy the godless nations with the words of his mouth. At his rebuke, nations will flee before him, and he will reprove sinners for the thoughts of their hearts.

He will gather together a pious people, to whom he will teach justice, He will judge the tribes of the people that have been sanctified by the Lord his god. He will not allow unlawfulness to remain anymore among them, nor will there remain with them any man who knows wickedness, for he will know them, that they are all sons of their god. He will divide them according to their tribes on the land, Neither traveler nor foreigner will stay with them anymore. He will judge peoples and nations in the wisdom of his lawfulness.

Psalm.

He will have the heathen nations to serve under his yoke, and he will praise the Lord in a place to be seen by all the Earth. He will purge Jerusalem, making it holy as in ancient times, so that nations will come from the egdes of the earth to see his glory, bringing as gifts her sons who had been taken, and to see the glory of the Lord, once God has glorified her.

He will be a righteous king over them, teaching about God. There will be no unlawfulness among them in his days, for all will be sacred and their king the anointed of the Lord. For he will not put his trust in horse, rider, and bow, nor will he amass for himself gold and silver for war. He will not make treaties with many for the day of battle, as the Lord himself is his king, and the trust in him is mighty, through his trust in God.

All nations will be afraid of being before him, for he will conquer the Earth forever with the words of his mouth. He will bless the people of the Lord with wisdom and joy, and he will be pure from sin, so that he may rule a great people. He will rebuke rulers, and remove sinners by the might of his words, relying on his god throughout his days. He will not stumble, for God will make him strong in spirit, holy, and wise in decisions, consistent with strength and justice.

The blessing of the Lord will be with him, and he will be strong and not stumble. His trust will be in the Lord, so who then can prevail against him? He will be mighty in his actions and strong in the fear of God. He will shepherd the flock of the Lord faithfully and righteously and will allow none among them to stumble in their pasture. He will lead them all correctly, and there will be no prideful among them who will oppress.

This will be the majesty of the king of Israel who God knows. He will elevate him over the house of Israel to correct them. His words will be more refined than the choicest, expensive gold. In the assemblies, he will judge the people of the tribes of the sanctified. His words will be like the words of the holy ones among the sanctified people. Blessed are those who will live in those days, in that they will see the good fortune of Israel which God will cause to happen in the gathering together of the tribes. May the Lord quickly bring his mercy on Israel! May he deliver us from the uncleanness of unlawful enemies! The Lord himself is our king forever and ever.

Psalms of Solomon: Chapter 18

'The Return of the Chosen of the Lord,' a Psalm of Solomon.

Lord, your mercy is in the works of your hands forever, and your goodness is over Israel with a rich gift. Your eyes look on them so that none of them are in need, and your ears listen to the hopeful prayer of the poor. Your judgments are executed on the whole Earth in mercy, and your love is toward the descendants of Abraham, the Israelites. Your punishment is on us as on a first-born, only-begotten son, to turn back the obedient mind from folly that is worked in ignorance. May God cleanse Israel against the day of mercy and blessing, against the day of decision, when those who will exist in those days will be blessed and he brings back his chosen. They will see the goodness of the Lord, which he will perform for the generation that is to come, under the cane of punishment of the Lord's chosen in the fear of God, his Sophia, spirit, justice, and strength, that he may direct every man in the action of lawfulness through the fear of God. He may establish them all before the Lord, a good generation living in the fear of God on the days of mercy.

Psalm.

Great and glorious is our god, living in the heights. It is he who has established in their courses the lights of the sky for determining seasons from year to year, and they have not turned aside from the way which he appointed them. In the fear of God, they pursue their path every day, from the day God created them and forever. They have not erred since the day he created them. Since the ancient generations, they have not deviated from their path, unless God commanded them to do so through the command of his servants.

Septuagint Manuscripts

The following is a list of the Septuagint manuscripts referenced in the notes for this book.

LXX א (Codex Sinaiticus) is dated to the 4th century. Parts of it are currently located at the British Library (Add. 43725) in London, Leipzig University (Gr. 1) in Leipzig, the National Library of Russia (Gr. 2, Gr. 259, Gr. 843, Fonds. d. Ges. f. alte Lit., and Oct 156) in Saint Petersburg, and Saint Catherine's Monastery (Neus Slg. МГ 1) on Mount Sinai.

LXX B (Codex Vaticanus) is dated to the 4th century. It is currently located at the Vatican Library (Gr. 1209) in Vatican City.

LXX V (Codex Venetus) is dated to the 8th century. It is currently located at the Vatican Library (Vat. Gr. 2106) in Vatican City and Biblioteca Marciana (Gr. 1) in Venice.

LXX 149 is dated to the 11th century. It is currently located at the Austrian National Library (Theol. gr. 11) in Vienna.

LXX 261 dates to 1323. It is currently located at the Laurentian Library (Plut. VII 30) in Florence.

LXX 766 is dated to the 12th century. It is currently located at the Great Lavra Monastery (Λαύρα, 355) on Mount Athos.

Alternative Translations

The following is a list of alternative translations that were used for comparative analysis.

The Aleppo Codex is dated to circa 920 AD. For centuries it was housed at the Central Synagogue of Aleppo, from which its name is derived. It was the oldest known complete copy of the Hebrew scriptures used within Judaism until 1947 when it was seized and divided among Jewish families during anti-Jewish riots in Aleppo. The sections that have resurfaced are currently at the Israel Museum in Jerusalem. Approximately 40% is still missing.

The Leningrad Codex is dated to 1008 (or 1009) AD. It is currently located at the National Library of Russia (Firkovich B 19 A) in St. Petersburg. The Leningrad Codex is the oldest complete copy of the Hebrew scriptures used within Judaism.

The Aramaic Targus to Proverbs, Ecclesiastes, and Song of Songs is generally accepted as having been compiled between 1 and 600 AD, although the surviving copies are all in Babylonian Aramaic.

Dead Sea Scrolls

The following is a list of the Dead Sea Scrolls mentioned in the notes for this book. Most are held by the Israel Museum in Jerusalem.

DSS 4Q102 (4QProv[a]) dates to the Herodian Dynasty (37 BC to 6 AD).

DSS 4Q103 (4QProv[b]) dates to the Herodian Dynasty (37 BC to 6 AD).

DSS 4Q110 (4QQoh[b]) is dated to the Herodian Dynasty in Judea (37 BC to 6 AD).

DSS 4Q106 (4QCant[a]) is dated to the Herodian Dynasty in Judea (37 BC to 6 AD).

DSS 4Q107 (4QCant[b]) is dated to the Herodian Dynasty in Judea (37 BC to 6 AD).

DSS 6Q6 (6QCant[a]) is dated to the Herodian Dynasty in Judea (37 BC to 6 AD)

Also Available

ALSO AVAILABLE

ENOCH AND METATRON SERIES:
- Books of Enoch Collection

- Books of Enoch and Metatron Collection

- Books of Metatron Collection

- Secrets of Enoch

OTHER TRANSLATIONS:
- Apocalypses of Ezra

- Arabic Maccabees

- Hebrew Maccabees

- Life of Adam and Eve

- Memories of the New Kingdom

- Septuagint's Esther and the Vetus Latina Esther

- Septuagint's Ezekiel and the Ba'al Cycle

- Septuagint's Job and the Testament of Job

- Septuagint's Proverbs and the Wisdom of Amenemope

- Syriac Maccabees – Deuterocanonical Books

- The Amarna Letters

- Testaments of the Patriarchs Collection

- Tobit and Ahikar

- Ugaritic Texts: Ba'al Cycle

- Wisdom of Ahikar

www.ingramcontent.com/pod-product-compliance
Lightning Source LLC
Chambersburg PA
CBHW060922120626
46557CB00003B/841